PEABODY
JOURNAL
OF EDUCATION

Camilla Benbow, Dean, Peabody College
James Guthrie, Editor
Jason Walton, Associate Editor
Rosie Moody, Coordinating Editor

T0346586

First published by Lawrence Erlbaum Associates, Inc., Publishers
10 Industrial Avenue
Mahwah, New Jersey 07430

Reprinted 2008 by Routledge

Routledge
Taylor & Francis Group
270 Madison Avenue
New York, NY 10016

Routledge
Taylor & Francis Group
2 Park Square
Milton Park, Abingdon
Oxon OX14 4RN

Send special requests for permission to the Permissions Department, Lawrence Erlbaum Associates, Inc., 10 Industrial Avenue, Mahwah, NJ 07430–2262.

Journal Project Supervisor: Mary A. Araneo, Lawrence Erlbaum Associates, Inc.

PEABODY
JOURNAL
OF EDUCATION

Volume 77, Number 2, 2002

Contemporary Issues in Psychological and Educational Assessment

(Continued)

PEABODY JOURNAL OF EDUCATION, 77(2), 1

Dedication

H. Carl Haywood

A Special Issue on

Contemporary Issues in Psychological and Educational Assessment

in honor of

Lloyd M. Dunn and

the late Leota Dunn

and in acknowledgment of their contributions
to psychological and educational assessment

PEABODY JOURNAL OF EDUCATION, 77(2), 3–5

Assessing Assessment: The Right Time, the Right Place, and the Right Reason

H. Carl Haywood
Peabody College
Vanderbilt University

Assessment of individual differences has been a major focus in psychology, especially educational psychology, for a full century. Over the last 100 years, psychologists and educators have learned to do that job, and in very many areas they have learned to do it quite well. In spite of our successes, the century mark seems a good time to assess areas still in need of improvement. Further, the success of psychometrics has taken us to a new inflection point in the progress curve in this field, a time when we can use the past as a starting point for future development. In this special issue of the *Peabody Journal of Education*, we take a broad look at the enterprise of assessment of individual differences in several domains. We do not expect to be exhaustive, but perhaps we can hope to be representative.

Assessment of individual differences began with efforts to distinguish degrees of difference in intelligence, which continues to be a major theme today. It has hardly been an exclusive theme, however. It is even possible that the concept of *intelligence* has outlived its usefulness—but that is another story! At least equal in importance to the assessment of individual differences in intelligence is the assessment of learning progress, as well as the assessment of personality differences, motivational differences, differences in language, and other cognitive development. In this issue we present the broad range of the field of psycho-educational assessment.

Requests for reprints should be sent to H. Carl Haywood, 144 Brighton Close, Nashville, TN 37205.

From a historical perspective, Peabody College of Vanderbilt University is an ideal place to undertake this enterprise. The first chairman of the department of psychology on the present campus (1914–1917) was E. K. Strong, Jr., whose principal fame derived from his development of a method of assessing individual differences in vocational interests. Joseph Peterson, who, in 1925, published an influential text on race differences in intelligence, succeeded Strong. In the 1950s and 1960s, Lloyd Dunn, chairman of the department of special education and one of the founders of the John F. Kennedy Center, developed a method of using relatively narrow-band operations to assess relatively broad-band constructs, resulting in the Peabody Picture Vocabulary Test. Dunn subsequently broadened his contributions to assessment with the Peabody Individual Achievement Test, which arose from the need for tests of scholastic achievement with sufficient range to be useful in the study of mental retardation and developmental disabilities. Julian Stanley, an international leader in psychometrics both from the standpoint of his studies of gifted learners and from his expertise in the mathematical treatment of individual differences data, was an important part of Peabody's psychometric history. The tradition continues to this day, with a persistent emphasis on individual differences in the study of mental retardation and, at the other end of the intelligence curve, the study of gifted learners, as well as the study of the development and education of children who have special educational needs.

With Peabody College having such a strong history in the field of psychometrics, it should have been no surprise that when I began to assemble this special issue, I continually encountered people who had been or are present members of the Peabody College faculty or who had earned doctoral degrees from Peabody. As it turned out, every paper in this special issue has at least one author who fits that description! Richard Woodcock was a professor of special education during the first golden age (the 1960s) of that department at Peabody and has returned as a visiting professor and the first occupant of the Lloyd and Leota Dunn chair in psychometrics. Lynn and Doug Fuchs are professors of special education at Peabody. David Tzuriel, a professor in the School of Education at Bar Ilan University in Israel, earned his PhD at Peabody. Sabine Wingenfeld, a psychology professor at La Trobe University in Australia, also earned her PhD in psychology at Peabody. Robert Bruininks, executive vice president and provost of the University of Minnesota, earned his PhD in special education at Peabody. Carl Haywood, now a professor of psychology, *emeritus*, was a member of the psychology faculty from 1962 to 1993, of the special education faculty during the 1970s, and served as director of the John F. Kennedy Center from 1971 to 1983. Steve Camarata is associate professor of Hearing and Speech and served as acting director of the John F. Kennedy Center from 2000 to 2002. Dan Reschley is professor and chair of Peabody's Department of Special Education. In fact, this collection of authors does not nearly exhaust the supply of Peabody-affiliated scholars whose work is and has been important to psychological and educational assessment; it represents a subset of that group whose work happened to fit the themes of this special issue and who were available to contribute to it.

The right reason? What better reason for a special issue on psychological and educational assessment than to honor Lloyd Dunn and the late Leota Dunn. The passing of Leota Dunn last fall gave impetus to this effort, whose time had come in any event. This special issue is one way for their colleagues to acknowledge and value the contributions of the Dunns to this field that is of such continuing importance. We are grateful to them for their work over so many years. We are also grateful to the editorial staff and publisher of the *Peabody Journal of Education* for giving us this opportunity.

PEABODY JOURNAL OF EDUCATION, 77(2), 6–22

New Looks in the Assessment of Cognitive Ability

Richard W. Woodcock
Peabody College
Vanderbilt University

The past 30 years have produced major changes in the measurement of cognitive ability and the interpretation of assessment results. Theory describing the factorial structure of cognitive ability has blossomed, and the results are visible in several recently published batteries of intellectual ability. The application of better theory to new assessment instruments has been facilitated by advances in the psychometric and statistical tools available to test developers. Attention is drawn to a concern about the capability of many clinicians to appreciate the importance of these changes and to apply them in practice without adequate continuing education.

The primary purpose for cognitive testing should be to find out more about the problem, not to obtain an IQ (Woodcock, 1997). It is essential that clinicians be aware of the major theoretical advances occurring in their field and appreciate the benefit to their assessment responsibilities accruing from the use of modern instruments reflecting those advances. Toward this end, two topics are addressed: (a) A review of the major conceptualizations of intelligence is presented, emphasizing recent advances in cognitive theory; and (b) information is provided about some recent advances in the statistical tools used by test developers that have greatly aided their work.

I wish to thank Fredrick Schrank and Kevin McGrew for their many helpful suggestions and critique of the manuscript.

Requests for reprints should be sent to Richard Woodcock, Peabody College, Box 40, 230 Appleton Place, Vanderbilt University, Nashville, TN 37203-5701.

Advances in Theory

Conceptualizations of Intelligence

There has been a clear trend in views of intelligence, from the simple to the more complex, as evidenced by the theoretical and interpretive models applied to tests of intelligence. The concept of a single, general intellectual ability dominated test development and interpretation for the first half of the 20th century. The beginning of the 21st century has witnessed the identification of a sizable set of specific, or narrow, cognitive abilities that underlie broader categories of human intellectual abilities. The history of cognitive abilities theory can be subdivided into five broad conceptualizations:

1. Intelligence as a single general ability
2. Intelligence as a pair of abilities
3. Intelligence as a limited set of multiple abilities
4. Intelligence as a complete set of multiple abilities
5. Intelligence as a hierarchy of narrow abilities underlying multiple broad abilities

Historically, the conceptualization of intelligence held by clinicians is intimately entwined with the major intelligence batteries available for their use. This is documented in Figure 1 through the portrayal of the relationship between level of conceptualization and the publication date of numerous major intelligence batteries available since 1916. Generally, a new level of conceptualization among clinicians has followed the publication of a particular intelligence battery, in turn, followed by the publication of other batteries based on a similar level of conceptualization. It is not likely that new intelligence batteries have ever grown from a recognition among clinicians that their current instruments were inadequate. Clinicians, by and large, tend to be consumers, not producers, of tests and interpretive models. Until recently, the mechanics of test administration were emphasized over theory in many professional preparation programs. Theory and research providing empirical support for test interpretation have had little effect on most clinician's evaluations of the adequacy of the instruments they use. For example, clinical lore has suggested that one of the factors identified in the Wechsler Intelligence Scale for Children (WISC–III) could be interpreted as a measure of freedom from distractibility even though no such cognitive ability has been independently verified, and many clinicians continue to interpret freedom from distractibility as a factor of intellectual ability. When advances are

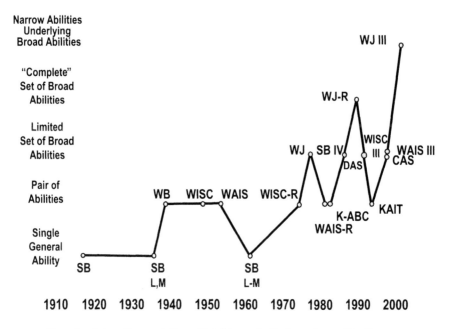

Figure 1. Interactive evolution of intelligence batteries and cognitive theory.

made practicable in the form of a measurement model, such as a theoretically based test battery, however, many clinicians can and do make changes in their conceptualizations, especially when the measurement model provides increased diagnostic capabilities and relevance to real-world interpretation.

Level 1: Intelligence as a single general ability. The earliest conceptualization of intelligence among clinicians, and still popular among some, at least operationally, is the view of intelligence as a single general ability. The Stanford–Binet (SB) test of 1916 (Terman, 1916) articulated that view of intelligence in the United States. Twenty-one years later, a revised SB was published with two alternate forms (Terman & Merrill, 1937). The third edition was published in 1960 (Terman & Merrill, 1960) as a single form that included the better test items from the previous two 1937 forms. Two scores were provided by these early SB tests: a mental age (MA) and a ratio IQ. The ratio IQ was obtained by dividing the MA by the subject's chronological age (CA). In the eyes of most clinicians using the early SB tests, that single IQ score represented all that was to be known about a person's intelligence. It should be noted, however, that the early SB tests included a rich variety of test items. Many examiners studied the pattern of correct and incorrect responses among the subject's responses to the various test items for clues about the nature of individual differences, or strengths and weaknesses in cognitive performance.

Level 2: Intelligence partitioned as a pair of abilities.   At Level 2, intelligence is perceived and measured as a pair of abilities, somewhat the opposite of each other (e.g., verbal versus nonverbal). This shift in the conceptualization of intelligence among clinicians primarily occurred following publication of the Wechsler–Bellevue (WB) in 1939 (Wechsler, 1939) and several subsequent versions of the Wechsler scales. In the eyes of most users, the WB was perceived as a measure of general intelligence or full scale IQ (FSIQ), undergirded by two narrower abilities, verbal IQ (VIQ) and performance IQ (PIQ).

The WB was a scale for adults. The first WISC was published in 1949 (Wechsler, 1949) and the Wechsler Adult Intelligence Scale (WAIS), replacing the WB, was published in 1955 (Wechsler, 1955). Clinicians now had a Wechsler available for use with children and another for use with adults. Both provided VIQ and PIQ scores plus an FSIQ. These two batteries were revised and released in 1974 and 1981 as the WISC–R (Wechsler, 1974) and the WAIS–R (Wechsler, 1981) with relatively little change from their earlier editions, quite possibly because little attention was paid to cognitive ability theory, at least among clinicians and the developers of the Wechsler scales, during these decades.

Other well-known tests associated with a Level 2 conceptualization include the Kaufman Assessment Battery for Children (K–ABC; Kaufman & Kaufman, 1983) and the Kaufman Adolescent & Adult Intelligence Test (KAIT; Kaufman & Kaufman, 1993). The K–ABC provides scales of simultaneous processing and sequential processing. The KAIT provides scales of crystallized and fluid intelligence.

Level 3: Intelligence as a limited set of multiple abilities.   The third level of conceptualization reflects the advent and subsequent use of intelligence batteries measuring more than two broad cognitive abilities. The first major battery to break with the pairing tradition established by the Wechsler scales was the Woodcock–Johnson Tests of Cognitive Abilities (WJ; Woodcock & Johnson, 1977). The WJ provided scores for four broad cognitive functions, identified as verbal ability, reasoning, perceptual speed, and memory.

The next Level 3 battery, published in 1986, was the Stanford–Binet Intelligence Scale, Fourth Edition (SB IV; Thorndike, Hagen, & Sattler, 1986). That battery also measured four broad categories of abilities: verbal reasoning, quantitative reasoning, abstract/visual reasoning, and short-term memory. Other Level 3 batteries published since 1986 include the Differential Abilities Scales (DAS; Elliot, 1990) measuring three broad categories (verbal, nonverbal reasoning, and spatial) and the WISC–III (Wechsler, 1991) measuring four broad categories (verbal comprehension, perceptual organization, freedom from distraction, and processing speed). The WISC–III was the first Wechsler battery to move beyond a Level 2 conceptualization of intelligence. The Cognitive Assessment System (CAS; Naglieri & Das, 1997) measures four separate functions (planning, attention, simultaneous processing, and successive processing). The WAIS–III (Wechsler, 1997) measures four abilities (verbal comprehension, perceptual organization, working memory, and processing speed).

Level 4: Intelligence as a complete set of broad cognitive abilities.   The next step advancing clinicians' conceptualizations of intelligence is associated with the availability of intelligence batteries intended to measure the complete set of broad abilities. Many contemporary scholars of intelligence would agree that the structure of cognitive ability is best portrayed by the Cattell–Horn–Carroll (CHC) theory of cognitive abilities. The CHC theory is an amalgamation of Cattell and Horn's Gf–Gc theory (Cattell, 1941; Horn, 1965, 1991; Horn & Noll, 1997) and Carroll's (1993, 1998) three-stratum theory of intelligence (Carroll & Horn, personal communication, July 1999).

The 1989 revision of the Woodcock–Johnson Tests of Cognitive Ability (WJ–R; Woodcock & Johnson, 1989b) measures seven broad abilities identified by the CHC theory. Two other broad abilities, quantitative knowledge and reading–writing, are measured as part of the companion achievement battery (Woodcock & Johnson, 1989a). The WJ–R was based on the Gf–Gc theory, now subsumed in the CHC theory.

Table 1 lists and describes nine well-defined CHC broad abilities. The acronyms presented for each broad ability are standard in the literature, though some writers may use variations. To add emphasis to the point that the purpose of testing should be to find out more about the problem, examples of implications from deficits in each of the nine abilities are included in the table.

Level 5: Cognitive ability as broad abilities undergirded by numerous narrow abilities.   This level of conceptualization recognizes that 60 or more nar-

Table 1

Description of Nine Cattel–Horn–Carroll (CHC) Broad Abilities

CHC Broad Ability	Description	Implications of Deficits
Acquired knowledge:		
Comprehension–knowledge (Gc)	The breadth and depth of knowledge, including verbal communication, information, and reasoning when using previously learned procedures.	Lacks information, language skills, and knowledge of procedures.
Quantitative knowledge (Gq)	The ability to comprehend quantitative concepts and relationships; the facility to manipulate numerical symbols.	Difficulty with arithmetic and other numerical tasks; poor at handling money and making change.
Reading–writing (Grw)	An ability in areas common to both reading and writing; probably includes basic reading and writing skills, and the *skills* required for comprehension and expression.	Difficulty with word attack, reading comprehension, or other basic reading skills; writing is inconsistent and characterized by errors of spelling and usage and of poor expression.
Thinking abilities:		
Long-term retrieval (Glr)	The ability to efficiently store information and retrieve it later.	Difficulty in recalling relevant information and in learning and retrieving names; needs more practice and repetition to learn than peers; inconsistent in remembering previously learned material.
Visual-spatial thinking (Gv)	Spatial orientation, with the ability to analyze and synthesize visual stimuli and to hold and manipulate mental images.	Poor spatial orientation; misperception of object–space relationships; difficulty with art and using maps; tendency to miss subtle social and interpersonal cues.

(Continued)

Table 1 *(Continued)*

CHC Broad Ability	Description	Implications of Deficits
Auditory processing (Ga)	The ability to discriminate, analyze, and synthesize auditory stimuli.	Speech discrimination problems; poor phonological knowledge; failure in recognizing sounds; increased likelihood of misunderstanding complex verbal instructions.
Fluid reasoning (Gf)	The ability to reason and solve problems often involving unfamiliar information or procedures, which is manifested in the reorganization, transformation, and extrapolation of information.	Difficulty in grasping abstract concepts, generalizing rules, and seeing implications; has difficulty changing strategies if first approach does not work.
Cognitive efficiency: Processing speed (Gs)	Speed and efficiency in performing automatic or very simple cognitive tasks.	Slow in executing easy cognitive tasks; slow acquisition of new material; tendency to become overwhelmed by complex events; needs extra time in responding to well-practiced tasks.
Short-term memory (Gsm)	The ability to hold information in immediate awareness and then use it within a few seconds.	Difficulty in remembering just-imparted instructions or information; easily overwhelmed by complex or multistep verbal directions.

row abilities underlie the 9 broad abilities described in Table 1. The narrow abilities represent qualitatively different specialized abilities that have been rather well defined in the literature. Horn (1991, pp. 207–223) relates the concept of narrow abilities to the primary mental abilities concept (Thurstone, 1938) and to well-replicated cognitive factors (WERCOF) primary abilities (Ekstrom, French, & Harmon, 1979). This is followed by Horn's presentation of several kinds of measures that are associated with each of 9 broad Gf–Gc abilities. Carroll (1993) identifies narrow abilities as in the first stratum of his three-stratum theory. The WJ–III (Woodcock, McGrew, & Mather, 2001a, 2001b) is a Level 5 battery. Each of the broad CHC abilities is measured by at least two qualitatively different narrow ability tests. Some 21 narrow abilities are documented as measured in the WJ–III Tests of Cognitive Ability and 19 other narrow abilities are measured in the WJ–III Tests of Achievement.

Table 2 provides several examples of narrow abilities associated with each of the broad CHC abilities. The acronyms listed for the narrow abilities in Table 2 are rather standard in the literature. Comprehension–knowledge (Gc) is an example of a broad ability with a list of underlying narrow abilities (e.g., language development, listening ability, and general information). Each narrow ability is a verifiably separate and measurable aspect of broad comprehension–knowledge and provides qualitatively different information. An examinee may demonstrate a significant strength or weakness on one of the measures but not on the others. A parallel can be drawn with the assessment of reading, a broad area of achievement. A variety of reading tests may be administered, each assessing a different narrow reading ability (e.g., word attack, word identification, or reading comprehension). To find out more about a reading problem, it may be necessary to measure several narrow aspects of reading so that the nature of the problem can be determined and appropriate instruction planned. The same strategy applies to the assessment of a problem in one of the broad cognitive abilities. A thorough discussion of narrow abilities and their measurement is presented in the *Intelligence Test Desk Reference* (ITDR; McGrew & Flanagan, 1998). Other useful references include Flanagan and Ortiz (2001) and Flanagan, McGrew, and Ortiz (2000).

The Cognitive and Academic Performance Model

An individual's observed cognitive and academic performance results from a complex interaction of many components. These components may be assigned to four broad categories differentiated by function: stores of acquired knowledge, thinking abilities, cognitive efficiency,

Table 2

Examples of Cattell–Horn–Carroll (CHC) Narrow Abilities

CHC Broad Ability	CHC Narrow Abilities
Acquired knowledge:	
Comprehension–knowledge (Gc)	Language development (LD)
	Lexical knowledge (VL)
	Listening ability (LS)
	Oral production and fluency (OP)
	General information (K0)
	Information about culture (K2)
Quantitative knowledge (Gq)	Mathematical achievement (A3)
	Mathematical knowledge (KM)
Reading–writing (Grw)	Reading decoding (RD)
	Reading comprehension (RC)
	Spelling ability (SG)
	Writing ability (WA)
	English usage knowledge (EU)
Thinking abilities:	
Long-term retrieval (Glr)	Associative memory (MA)
	Meaningful memory (MM)
	Figural fluency (FF)
	Ideational fluency (FI)
	Naming facility (NA)
Visual–spatial thinking (Gv)	Visualization (Vz)
	Spatial relations (SR)
	Flexibility of closure (CF)
	Length estimation (LE)
	Visual memory (MV)
	Spatial scanning (SS)
Auditory processing (Ga)	Phonetic coding (PC)
	Speech-sound discrimination (US)
	General sound discrimination (U3)
	Resistance to auditory stimulus distortion (UR)
Fluid feasoning (Gf)	Induction (I)
	General sequential reasoning (RG)
	Memory for sound patterns (UM)
	Quantitative reasoning (RQ)
Cognitive efficiency:	
Processing speed (Gs)	Perceptual speed (P)
	Semantic processing speed (R4)
	Rate of test taking (R9)
	Number facility (N)
Short-term memory (Gsm)	Working memory (WM)
	Memory span (MS)

and facilitator–inhibitors. These categories are logically derived, based on similar and dissimilar characteristics. Each of these four categories includes components that contribute in a common way to cognitive performance but also contribute differently from the common contribution of the other three categories. Figure 2 illustrates the relationship between the four functional categories and cognitive/academic performance.

In the cognitive and academic performance model, the fourth oval represents the influence of facilitator–inhibitors. These are the noncognitive factors that modify cognitive and academic performance for better or worse, often overriding the effects of strengths and weaknesses in the individual's cognitive and achievement profiles. The source of some facilitator–inhibitors is internal (e.g., health, emotional state, and motivation/volition), while the source of other facilitator–inhibitors is situational and environmental (e.g., the presence of visual and auditory distractions, the response format, or the types of tests selected for a cognitive examination).

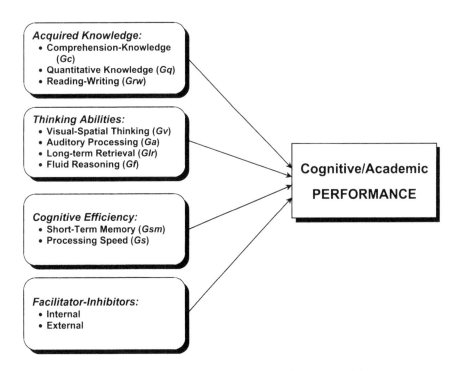

Figure 2. The cognitive and academic performance model.

There are several ways in which the cognitive performance model can be helpful in interpretation of the CHC broad and narrow abilities. Grouping the broad abilities by similarities can help practitioners understand some practical implications of test performance. For example, the stores of acquired knowledge include Gc, quantitative knowledge (Gq), and reading–writing ability (Grw). All of these abilities are learned. Once a piece of information is learned, it can become a building block for new learning. Similarly, if a piece of information is not learned, it can become an impediment to future learning. Additionally, the stores of acquired knowledge are mutable; that is, teaching strategies and enrichment opportunities can impact an individual's performance levels.

The thinking abilities are the processes through which new learning occurs. These processes include visual–spatial thinking (Gv), auditory processing (Ga), long-term retrieval (Glr), and fluid reasoning (Gf). Limitations in one or more of these thinking abilities will likely constrain new learning, possibly requiring alternative forms of instruction. Also, new learning will be constrained by any limitations in the relevant stores of acquired knowledge.

Cognitive efficiency includes short-term memory (Gsm) and processing speed (Gs). Automatic cognitive performance will be constrained by any limitations in these broad abilities. Lowered levels of cognitive efficiency frequently require accommodations in instruction and in activities such as group testing situations.

All performance, especially new learning, is constrained by any limitations among the facilitator–inhibitors. For example, uncorrected poor visual acuity will likely result in missed opportunities for learning. Any significant health problems that result in poor school attendance can disrupt learning opportunities. Poor motivation to learn, or low interest in academics, will likely affect academic task engagement. Certain cognitive style or temperament characteristics, such as impulsivity, can negatively affect the quality of one's work. Other factors, such as emotional stability, organization, and ability to concentrate, can positively or negatively affect learning opportunities. Consequently, the depiction of this broad class of facilitator–inhibitors as a component of cognitive performance can help practitioners to pay greater attention to these variables when evaluating an individual's cognitive and/or academic performance.

Other, more complex and informative, models of cognitive performance based on the CHC theory include the Gf–Gc Information Processing Model (Woodcock, 1993) and the Cognitive Neuropsychology Model (Dean & Woodcock, 1999, 2003; Woodcock, 1998).

Advances in Statistical and Test Development Tools

Advances in their statistical tools of trade have impacted the work of cognitive theorists and intelligence test developers. For the theorist, the most notable among these advances has likely been the development of powerful confirmatory factor analysis programs. For the test developer, item response theory (IRT), better procedures for the imputation of missing data, and the availability of complex curve-fitting programs have transformed their approach to the task.

Tools Applied to Cognitive Theory

Toward the advancement of cognitive theory, among the most useful tools are confirmatory factor analysis (CFA) programs (e.g., LISREL, AMOS, M-PLUS, EQS). These computer programs, which are largely based on the iterative power of maximum-likelihood analysis, have enhanced efforts toward describing the factorial structure of human cognitive abilities. Included in these programs are procedures for evaluating the comparative fit of competing measurement models, a feature that provides for a degree of objectivity in the hands of sophisticated users.

CFA methods are used during various stages of test development. First, theory-driven CFA methods have been applied to published editions of intelligence and achievement batteries to ascertain how an existing battery of tests measures, or does not measure, certain abilities according to a specific cognitive theory. The results are then used to specify a revision plan that will result in a battery of tests better representing the major domains specified by the theory. Once data gathering has begun, CFAs performed on early processed data can assist test developers in determining if new or revised tests are behaving as expected (i.e., loading on the factor constructs they were designed to measure). Revisions to tests, or the development of new tests, can then occur prior to gathering the majority of the norm data. Finally, CFA analysis at the end of a test norming project provides important structural validity information in support of the organizational structure of a battery of tests.

Though not a statistical program in itself, *joint factor analysis* can assist in identifying the subset of CHC broad and narrow abilities measured by an intelligence battery that does not contain at least two or three separate measures for each factor implicit in the battery. In an early joint factor analysis study that employed both exploratory and confirmatory factor analysis techniques, Woodcock (1990, 1994) investigated the factorial structure of six widely used, individually administered intelligence batteries. Two observations from that study are of interest here. First, it was demonstrated that the breadth of factor coverage in certain batteries was greater than reflected in the interpretation systems provided by the publishers. For example, the WISC–R provided verbal and performance scores, but Woodcock reported that the WISC–R tests measured five distinct CHC factors (Gc, Gq, Gv, Gs, and Gsm) lumped together into the two interpretive scores. Newer versions of the Wechslers provide interpretive schemes that more closely reflect CHC theory.

Second, the results of this study drew attention to the fact that different labeled abilities (and composite scores) across different intelligence batteries were often factorially equivalent even though their labels differed and clinicians perceived them as measuring different traits. For example, both the Wechsler perceptual organization and the K–ABC simultaneous processing scales were demonstrated to be measures of the same broad CHC ability, visual–spatial thinking (Gv). The K–ABC sequential processing scale was demonstrated to be a measure of short-term memory (Gsm). Clinicians need to be cognizant that tests with unique names that purport to measure unique traits may simply be new tests measuring well-established CHC factors. The most famous description of this property of names is perhaps Juliet's line to Romeo:

> What's in a name? that which we call a rose
> By any other name would smell as sweet.
> (Shakespeare, *Romeo and Juliet*)

Woodcock's early study led to a series of subsequent joint factor analysis studies, often called cross-battery studies. As a result, there now exists a classification of the individual tests from all major intelligence and achievement batteries within a common CHC nomenclature (see Flanagan et al., 2000; Flanagan & Ortiz, 2001; Flanagan, Ortiz, Alfonso, & Mascolo, 2002; McGrew, 1997; McGrew & Flanagan, 1998).

Tools Applied to Test Development

Arguably, the single most important advancement in psychometrics for the test developer has been the introduction of IRT (Embretson & Reise, 2000; Hambleton & Swaminathan, 1985). Particularly influential has been the Rasch model, a single-parameter logistic test model used to analyze item response data (Embretson, 1996; Rasch, 1960; Wright, 1968; Wright & Stone, 1979). Several benefits realized from the application of the Rasch model to test development include the following:

• Sample-free item calibration: Difficulty levels assigned to items are independent of the level and distribution of ability in the sample chosen to calibrate the items.

• Item-free measurement: After a bank of items fitting the model is calibrated, any subset of items may be used to construct a test and the ability scores from this new test will be on the same scale as the bank of items. As an example of this benefit, multiple forms of a test can be constructed easily on the same underlying measurement scale.

• Item difficulties and ability scores are on the same scale (Woodcock & Dahl, 1971). The distance on the scale between task difficulty and a person's ability provides a direct and quantifiable implication for performance on that task. This information can be generalized to the prediction of performance with similar tasks.

• The equating of tests is simplified, even across languages (Woodcock & Muñoz-Sandoval, 1993).

• Options for interpreting test performance are extended (Woodcock, 1999). For example, test performance can be reported as a criterion-referenced score that describes quality of performance or proficiency compared to others of the same age or grade, or as a developmental zone extending from a fixed level of easiness to a fixed level of difficulty for a given subject.

Missing data are the bane of existence for test developers and many applied researchers. By definition, all standard multivariate statistical methods (e.g., multiple regression or factor analysis) require a complete set of data on all variables in order for a subject's data to be included in the analyses. The absence of a score for a single variable can render 100% of that subject's available data useless. As a result, less accurate estimates of statistical parameters are obtained due to the reduced size of the database. Due, in many respects, to the increased availability of high-speed and low-cost computers, archaic improvisations such as replacing a missing score by the mean (mean substitution) or by the value of an adjacent subject are rarely used today. They have been replaced by procedures such as regression substitution, stochastic regression imputation, hot-deck imputation, multiple imputation, and maximum-likelihood methods (including the expectation maximization or EM algorithm).

A third significant advancement in test development tools is the emergence of better programs that facilitate the discovery of equations for complex curves that characterize large data sets. For example, the TableCurve 2D (Systat, 1997a) and TableCurve 3D (Systat, 1997b) programs are two- and three-dimensional curve- and surface-fitting programs. These programs readily accommodate missing data and generate sets of possible complex equations that provide the best possible fit of a curve or a surface to a large set of data. The use of such programs has had a major impact on the computation of norms for a test vis-à-vis (a) the reduction of human error present in earlier hand curve-fitting procedures, (b) the generation of sets of viable equations/curves from which to select, (c) the generation of a variety of fit statistics by which to evaluate solutions, (d) the ability to superimpose and visually compare multiple curve solutions, (e) the ability to apply *pre-smoothers* that reduce wild data points resulting from sampling error, and (f) the quick and efficient transfer of the final smoothed values and/or computer code to other software.

Conclusion

At the beginning of this article, it was stated that the primary purpose of a comprehensive cognitive assessment should be to gain information about the problem, not to obtain an IQ. Advances in cognitive theory, and the subsequent availability of intelligence batteries based on these advances, provide clinicians with knowledge and tools that are more informative and that allow for finer diagnostic interpretations. Tests of the future will become more informative but not necessarily more complex. As a consequence, it is incumbent on clinicians and the trainers of clinicians to stay abreast with advances in cognitive theory and measurement and with their corresponding implications for practice. Attention to these advances should not be limited to the primary training programs for clinicians but needs to be a major component of continuing professional education. All professionals—whether they are tax accountants, physicians, or educational/psychological clinicians—have an ethical responsibility to their clients to stay abreast of changes in their field.

References

Carroll, J. B. (1993). *Human cognitive abilities: A survey of factor-analytic studies.* Cambridge, England: Cambridge University Press.

Carroll, J. B. (1998). Human cognitive abilities: A critique. In J. J. McArdle & R. W. Woodcock (Eds.), *Human cognitive abilities in theory and practice* (pp. 5–23). Mahwah, NJ: Lawrence Erlbaum Associates, Inc.

Cattell, R. B. (1941). Some theoretical issues in adult intelligence testing. *Psychological Bulletin, 38,* 592.

Dean, R. S., & Woodcock, R. W. (1999). *The WJ–R and Batería–R in neuropsychological assessment: Research report number 3.* Itasca, IL: Riverside.

Dean, R. S., & Woodcock, R. W. (2003). *Dean–Woodcock Neuropsychological Assessment System.* Itasca, IL: Riverside.

Ekstrom, R. B., French, J. W., & Harmon, M. H. (1979). Cognitive factors: Their identification and replication. *Multivariate Behavioral Research Monographs, 79*(2).

Elliot, C. D. (1990). *Differential Abilities Scales.* San Antonio, TX: Psychological Corporation.

Embretson, S. E. (1996). The new rules of measurement. *Psychological Assessment, 8,* 341–349.

Embretson, S. E., & Reise, S. P. (2000). *Item response theory for psychologists.* Mahwah, NJ: Lawrence Erlbaum Associates, Inc.

Flanagan, D. P., McGrew, K. S., & Ortiz, S. O. (2000). *The Wechsler Intelligence Scales and G–Gc theory.* Boston: Allyn & Bacon.

Flanagan, D. P., & Ortiz, S. W. (2001). *Essentials of cross-battery assessment.* New York: Wiley.

Flanagan, D. P., Ortiz, S. W., Alfonso, V., & Mascolo, J. (2002). *The achievement test desk reference (ATDR): Comprehensive assessment and learning disabilities.* Boston: Allyn & Bacon.

Hambleton, R. K., & Swaminathan, H. (1985). *Item response theory: Principles and applications.* Norwell, MA: Kluwer Academic.

Horn, J. L. (1965). Fluid and crystallized intelligence. Unpublished doctoral dissertation, University of Illinois, Urbana–Champaign.

Horn, J. L. (1991). Measurement of intellectual capabilities: A review of theory. In K. S. McGrew, J. K. Werder, & R. W. Woodcock, *WJ–R technical manual* (pp. 197–232). Chicago: Riverside.

Horn, J. L., & Noll, J. (1997). Human cognitive capabilities: Gf–Gc theory. In D. P. Flanagan, J. L. Genshaft, & P. L. Harrison (Eds.), *Contemporary intellectual assessment: Theories, tests, and issues* (pp. 53–91). New York: Guilford.

Kaufman, A. S., & Kaufman N. L. (1983). *Kaufman Assessment Battery for Children.* Circle Pines, MN: American Guidance Service.

Kaufman, A. S., & Kaufman N. L. (1993). *The Kaufman Adolescent and Adult Intelligence Test.* Circle Pines, MN: American Guidance Service.

McGrew, K. S. (1997). Analysis of the major intelligence batteries according to a proposed comprehensive Gf–Gc framework. In D. P. Flanagan, J. L. Genshaft, & P. L. Harrison (Eds.), *Contemporary intellectual assessment: Theories, tests, and issues* (pp. 151–189). New York: Guilford.

McGrew, K. S., & Flanagan, D. P. (1998). *The intelligence test desk reference (ITDR): A cross-battery approach to intelligence test interpretation.* Boston: Allyn & Bacon.

Naglieri, J. A., & Das, J. P. (1997). *Cognitive assessment system.* Itasca, IL: Riverside.

Rasch, G. (1960). *Probabilistic models for some intelligence and attainment tests.* Copenhagen, Denmark: Danish Institute for Educational Research.

Systat (1997a). TableCurve 2D [Computer Software]. Richmond, CA: Systat Software.

Systat (1997b). TableCurve 3D [Computer Software]. Richmond, CA: Systat Software.

Terman, L. M. (1916). *The measurement of intelligence.* Boston: Houghton Mifflin.

Terman, L. M., & Merrill, M. A. (1937). *Measuring intelligence: A guide to the administration of the new revised Stanford-Binet tests of intelligence.* Boston: Houghton Mifflin.

Terman, L. M., & Merrill, M. A. (1960). *Stanford–Binet Intelligence Scale: Manual for the third revision. Form L–M.* Boston: Houghton Mifflin.

Thorndike, R. M., Hagen, E. P., & Sattler, J. M. (1986). *Stanford–Binet Intelligence Scale–Fourth Edition.* Itasca, IL: Riverside.

Thurstone, L. L. (1938). Primary mental abilities. *Psychometric Monographs, 1.*

Wechsler, D. (1939). *The measurement of adult intelligence.* Baltimore: Williams & Wilkins.

Wechsler, D. (1949). *Wechsler Intelligence Scale for Children.* San Antonio, TX: Psychological Corporation.

Wechsler, D. (1955). *Wechsler Adult Intelligence Scale.* San Antonio, TX: Psychological Corporation.

Wechsler, D. (1974). *Wechsler Intelligence Scale for Children–Revised*. San Antonio, TX: Psychological Corporation.

Wechsler, D. (1981). *Wechsler Adult Intelligence Scale–Revised*. San Antonio, TX: Psychological Corporation.

Wechsler, D. (1991). *Wechsler Intelligence Scale for Children–Third Edition*. San Antonio, TX: Psychological Corporation.

Wechsler, D. (1997). *Wechsler Adult Intelligence Scale–Third Edition*. San Antonio, TX: Psychological Corporation.

Woodcock, R. W. (1990). Theoretical foundations of the WJ–R measures of cognitive ability. *Journal of Psychoeducational Assessment, 8,* 231–258.

Woodcock, R. W. (1993). An information processing view of Gf–Gc theory. *Journal of Psychoeducational Assessment Monograph Series:* Advances in Psychoeducational Assessment, *Woodcock–Johnson Psycho-Educational Battery–Revised.* Brandon, VT: Clinical Psychology Publishing Company.

Woodcock, R. W. (1994). Measures of fluid and crystallized theory of intelligence. In R. J. Sternberg (Ed.), *Encyclopedia of human intelligence* (pp. 452–456). New York: Macmillan.

Woodcock, R. W. (1997). The Woodcock-Johnson Tests of Cognitive Ability—Revised. In D. P. Flanagan, J. L. Genshaft, & P. L. Harrison (Eds.), *Contemporary intellectual assessment: Theories, tests, and issues* (pp. 230–245). New York: Guilford.

Woodcock, R. W. (1998). *The WJ–R and Batería–R in neuropsychological assessment: Research report number 1.* Itasca, IL: Riverside.

Woodcock, R. W. (1999). What can Rasch-based scores convey about a person's test performance? In S. Embretson & S. Hershberger (Eds.), *The new rules of measurement: What every psychologist and educator should know* (pp. 105–127). Mahwah, NJ: Lawrence Erlbaum Associates, Inc.

Woodcock, R. W., & Dahl, M. N. (1971). *A common scale for the measurement of person ability and test item difficulty* (AGS Paper No. 10). Circle Pines, MN: American Guidance Service.

Woodcock, R. W., & Johnson, M. B. (1977). *Woodcock–Johnson Psycho-Educational Battery.* Itasca, IL: Riverside.

Woodcock, R. W., & Johnson, M. B. (1989a). *Woodcock–Johnson Tests of Achievement–Revised.* Itasca, IL: Riverside.

Woodcock, R. W., & Johnson, M. B. (1989b). *Woodcock–Johnson Tests of Cognitive Ability–Revised.* Itasca, IL: Riverside.

Woodcock, R. W., McGrew, K. S., & Mather, N. (2001a). *Woodcock–Johnson III Tests of Achievement.* Itasca, IL: Riverside.

Woodcock, R. W., McGrew, K. S., & Mather, N. (2001b). *Woodcock–Johnson III Tests of Cognitive Abilities.* Itasca, IL: Riverside.

Woodcock, R. W., & Muñoz-Sandoval, A. F. (1993). An IRT approach to cross-language test equating and interpretation. *European Journal of Psychological Assessment, 9,* 233–241.

Wright, B. D. (1968). Sample-free test calibration and person measurement. *Proceedings of the 1967 Invitational Conference on Testing Problems* (pp. 85–101). Princeton, NJ: Educational Testing Service.

Wright, B. D., & Stone, M. H. (1979). *Best test design.* Chicago: MESA Press.

PEABODY JOURNAL OF EDUCATION, 77(2), 23–39

Pieces of the Puzzle: Measuring the Personal Competence and Support Needs of Persons With Intellectual Disabilities

James R. Thompson
Department of Special Education
Illinois State University

Kevin S. McGrew and Robert H. Bruininks
Department of Special Education
University of Minnesota

Theoretical and empirical efforts to develop valid methods by which to identify people with mental retardation and related disabilities have been underway for approximately 100 years. Recently, there is a growing consensus that mental retardation is best conceptualized as significant limitations in the multidimensional construct of personal competence. In addition to physical competence, personal competence is conceptualized to include, at the broadest level of conceptualization, the domains of conceptual, practical, and social intelligence. Due to limitations in personal competence, the defining characteristic of persons with mental retardation is an ongoing need for types and intensities of support that most others in society do not require. Current models of personal competence are described and the types of measurement tools available to measure essential dimensions of personal

Requests for reprints should be sent to Jim Thompson, Associate Professor and Interim Chair, Department of Special Education, Illinois State University—Mail Code 5910, Normal, IL 61790–5910.

competence are discussed. Additionally, a systematic approach is described for assessing support needs and developing plans to meet these needs.

There is only one reality in psychology—the reality of individual differences. No two people are the same. People differ on physical, personality, and intellectual characteristics, and in a myriad of other ways. Individual differences make each person unique and provide for a diverse, heterogeneous society.

Individuals with advanced intellectual abilities are said to be *gifted* and in extreme cases are referred to as *geniuses*. Conversely, individuals who cannot complete common everyday cognitive tasks, or who can only complete them with partial success, are often said to be individuals with *mental retardation, cognitive delays,* or *intellectual disabilities*.

In this article, we examine issues pertaining to the identification and support needs of people with intellectual disabilities. Specifically, we (a) contend that there are compelling reasons to continue theoretical and empirically validated efforts to develop more reliable and valid methods by which to identify people with mental retardation, (b) review the historical evolution of the concept of mental retardation and the corresponding efforts to measure its critical dimensions, (c) propose that future conceptualizations of mental retardation be based on a multidimensional construct of personal competence, (d) present the need for valid instruments to measure key dimensions of personal competence, (e) propose that the focal point of service delivery systems should be on identifying and securing the supports that people with mental retardation need to experience an enjoyable quality of life, and (f) describe initial efforts to systematically measure individual support needs and develop individualized support plans.

Is It Justifiable to Identify People With Mental Retardation?

Prior to considering how to best identify people with mental retardation, it is critical to determine whether such an endeavor is justifiable. Ysseldyke, Algozzine, and Thurlow (1992) have made the point that disability categories are social constructions in that they are

constructs given meaning and life through comparison of performance to criteria. Blindness is a name assigned to visual performance judged different from that called average or normal. Giftedness and mental retardation are names assigned to intellectual performance judged different from that called average or normal. Criteria accepted as evidence for a condition form the cornerstones of a definition. Definition is the cornerstone for the existence of a condition. For all practical purposes, without definitions there are no categories. (p. 92)

Formal efforts to identify and differentiate people as a function of their lack of intellectual abilities and skills have been characterized by some as misguided due to the potential unintended effects of negative stereotypes and resultant discrimination (Danforth, 1997; Kliewer & Biklen, 1996). For example, in examining special education through a postmodernist lens, Danforth concluded that learning differences become artificially overstated through the use of disability categories. His position is that it is wrong to perpetuate a belief that "certain persons in society have a deficit condition called 'mental retardation' that requires professional intervention" (p. 99–100) and implies that if all children were viewed only as individual learners their needs would be accommodated by educators as a matter of course. According to Danforth, diagnosis is when "a child's social identity is quickly refashioned from 'normal' status to debilitated learner" (p. 101).

However, the dominant thinking in the fields of special education and mental retardation assumes that there are certain individuals within the population who need special assistance for improved learning and cultural adaptation. If not identified, they would be unable to receive the necessary education and other supports needed to reach their full potential. Although disability labels have the potential to adversely impact an individual, the bottom line is that "it is simply a logical impossibility to talk about students as having special needs without labeling them as having special needs" (Hockenbury, Kauffman, & Hallahan, 1999–2000, p. 5). Proponents of identification suggest that a person's difficulties in school achievement, learning, work, or community living are the true source of any *stigma*, and the benefits derived from special assistance outweighs any costs associated with the disability label (e.g., Kauffman, 1999; Lewis, Bruininks, Thurlow, & McGrew, 1989).

Our position is that the challenges people with mental retardation face on a daily basis are real and will not disappear if they were no longer identified as people with mental retardation. Because we believe that mental retardation is real, we endorse efforts to improve methods of identification that lead to effective interventions to increase learning and adaptation. Moreover, we believe it is essential to identify individuals with mental retardation so (a) they can receive services and supports that will enable them to live productive and fulfilling lives, (b) they can be legally protected from unfair treatment or exploitation, and (c) systematic research can be conducted that will yield knowledge that will ultimately lead to better systems of learning and support.

Personal Competence as the Defining
Feature of Mental Retardation

Definitions of mental retardation have changed over time. Because "definition is the cornerstone for the existence of a condition" (Ysseldyke et al., 1992, p. 92), every time there is a change in the definition of mental retardation, there is a corresponding change in the population of persons with mental retardation. People who meet criteria under one definition may not meet criteria under a revised one.

The history of defining mental retardation is instructive. Our study of this history has led us to the conclusion that mental retardation should be conceptualized as significant limitations in the conceptual, practical, and social dimensions of personal competence that creates a need for types of support that most others in society do not need. This conceptualization of mental retardation is largely consistent with previous conceptualizations offered by Greenspan (1999b), the American Association on Mental Retardation's Ad Hoc Committee on Terminology and Classification (Luckasson et al., 2002), and Schalock (2002). We predict that a multidimensional approach to personal competence and a focus on identifying support needs will characterize formal definitions of mental retardation in the coming years.

The Prominence of Personal Competence in Early
Conceptualizations of Mental Retardation

Early pioneers in the field of mental retardation (e.g., Itard, Seguin, Voison, and Howe) characterized people with mental retardation as being vulnerable and lacking personal independence due to deficits in social competency and a lack of practical skills needed to successfully adapt to the environment (Nihira, 1999). Moreover, early legal definitions of mental retardation emphasized deficits in community adaptation (Bruininks, Thurlow, & Gilman, 1987). Although tools to assess personal independence, social competence, practical skills, and community adaptation were not available to these early scholars beyond acute observation, it was clear that as the field of mental retardation began to emerge, there was initial consensus that people with mental retardation were different than others due to a significant difficulty in dealing with the demands of a complex world. Personal competence was, in many respects, the cornerstone of early definitions of mental retardation.

IQ Rises to Prominence

The introduction of Binet's intelligence test and the subsequent expansion of the intelligence testing movement during the early 1900s shifted attention away from indicators of the broad construct of personal competence to an exaggerated focus on IQ scores. Since it was assumed that people with mental retardation were different from the rest of the population by virtue of deficient intellectual functioning, the intelligence quotient was perceived as an objective and practical tool. The IQ test provided an efficient means by which to provide a clear and concrete indication of the degree an individual deviated from the general population (Scheerenberger, 1983; Smith, 1998). However, concerns over the narrowness of the behaviors sampled by IQ tests soon arose (e.g., see Doll, 1936; Tredgold, 1922) and eventually a steady stream of critiques led to efforts to broaden the assessment of behaviors in defining mental retardation (Scheerenberger, 1983).

Adaptive Behavior Comes on Board

Of the numerous definitions of mental retardation that emerged during the first half of the 20th century, Edgar Doll's 1941 definition had the most enduring impact. Doll indicated that the following six criteria were essential to understanding mental retardation: "(1) social incompetence, (2) due to mental subnormality, (3) which has been developmentally arrested, (4) which obtains at maturity, (5) is of constitutional origin, and (6) is essentially incurable" (Doll, 1941, p. 215). Smith (1998) pointed out that Doll's first four criteria have stood the test of time, but the last two have not. It is now widely recognized that environmental variables can contribute to delayed development and lower personal competence (Baumeister, Kupstas, & Woodley-Zanthos, 1993). Additionally, it is possible for an individual to achieve a level of personal competence where he or she is no longer significantly different from the rest of society to warrant a diagnosis of mental retardation (Luckasson et al., 2002). However, Doll was a visionary in that he understood the fundamental role the construct of social intelligence should play in the definition of mental retardation. For the past 25 years Stephen Greenspan and others have expanded Doll's construct of social intelligence in exploring the meaning of mental retardation. Greenspan has argued convincingly that components of personal competence associated with social intelligence have been overlooked in definitions of mental retardation (Greenspan, 1979; Greenspan & Driscoll, 1997; Greenspan & Granfield, 1992).

By the late 1950s, Doll and others had built a strong case against using the IQ score as the sole indicator of mental retardation. It was obvious that IQ tests were measures of certain circumscribed aspects of cognitive functioning related to academic tasks (i.e., linguistic, conceptual, and mathematical abilities and skills) that did not tap other aspects of personal competence that are essential for independent functioning (e.g., social intelligence and practical intelligence). Diagnostic decisions based exclusively on an IQ score ran the risk of being misguided due to insufficient information. In 1959, the American Association on Mental Deficiency (now known as the American Association on Mental Retardation, or AAMR) published a revised definition that specifically included deficits in adaptive behavior as a second criterion for the diagnosis of mental retardation (Heber, 1959). Intellectual functioning (as measured by IQ tests) and adaptive behavior (as measured by adaptive behavior scales) remain the two central features of definitions of mental retardation today (e.g., state and federal governmental definitions, international definitions, and definitions published by professional organizations).

From its introduction, the construct of adaptive behavior has been a source of considerable controversy. Adaptive behavior scales were generally applauded for their value in identifying explicit competencies of individuals with mental retardation in observable and measurable terms as such information was very useful when developing individualized educational and habilitation goals (Nihira, 1999). However, the usefulness of adaptive behavior scales in measuring broad aspects of personal competence has been questioned. For example, after more than a decade of including adaptive behavior criteria in definitions of mental retardation, Clausen (1972) claimed that the determination of mental retardation continued to be based almost exclusively on intelligence tests.

We believe that the fundamental problem that has plagued the development of adaptive behavior scales has been the absence of a consensual theoretical definition of the construct to be measured (i.e., adaptive behavior). Greenspan (1997) indicated that the construct of adaptive behavior "was devised in the absence of a model of competence; as a consequence it was operationally defined as a mishmash of practical intelligence (activities of daily living) and absence of psychopathology (good affective competence)" (pp. 140–141). Coulter and Morrow (1978) compared 10 definitions of adaptive behavior published between 1968 and 1976 and noted that no 2 definitions were alike (although there were similarities between many of the definitions). The plethora of different behavior scales that emerged throughout the 1970s and 1980s increased confusion over what exactly it was that adaptive behavior scales were measuring. Zigler, Balla, and Hodapp (1984) concluded that adaptive behavior was a meaningless construct because it was so unclear; they argued for a return to an IQ-only definition of mental retardation.

To better understand adaptive behavior, several researchers initiated factor analytic studies in an effort to identify and define the key dimensions (i.e., factors) of the construct (e.g., see Bruininks, McGrew, & Maruyama, 1988; Matson, Epstein, & Cullinan, 1984; Owens & Bowling, 1970; Sparrow & Cicchetti, 1978). In a review of 31 published factor analytic studies (reporting data from 86 independent samples and 9 different scales), Thompson, McGrew, and Bruininks (1999) concluded that adaptive behavior, as collectively measured by existing instruments, is a multidimensional construct that appears to consist of 5 broad domains of behavior, namely, personal independence, responsibility, cognitive/academic, physical/developmental, and vocational/community. Additionally, Thompson et al. concluded that no single adaptive behavior measurement scale comprehensively measured the entire range of adaptive behavior dimensions (e.g., 7 scales provided measures of personal independence but only 4 scales provided measures of social responsibility). Although this review, in conjunction with earlier reviews (see Meyers, Nirhira, & Zetlin, 1979; McGrew & Bruininks, 1989; Widaman, Borthwick-Duffy, & Little, 1991; Widaman & McGrew, 1996) helped clarify the factor structure adaptive behavior, the reviews also confirmed the definitional confusion that surrounds this construct. As a result, there are a plethora of adaptive behavior scales on the market today that measure many different things.

The AAMR's 1992 definition and classification manual (Luckasson et al., 1992) added further complexity to the debate over the meaning of adaptive behavior. In the 1992 AAMR manual, adaptive behavior was defined as consisting of 10 specific adaptive skill areas (communication, self-care, home living, social skills, community use, self-direction, health and safety, functional academics, leisure, and work). Moreover, the operational criterion for identifying mental retardation was the presence of limitations in 2 or more skill areas. Critics charged that the 10 areas of adaptive skills lacked theoretical and empirical justification and that there were no tools to assess all 10 areas at the time the 1992 manual was published (Jacobson & Mulik, 1992; MacMillan, Gresham, & Siperstein, 1993). These criticisms, plus others, resulted in Greenspan (1997) concluding that the 1992 AAMR manual "should be declared an honorable mistake and given a decent burial" (p. 179).

Personal Competence Rises Again

Although AAMR's 1992 manual (Luckason et al., 1992) had its detractors, certain aspects of the manual offered promise for a more comprehensive and functional conceptualization of mental retardation. For example, although the 10 adaptive skill areas may have lacked empirical validity, this top-10 skill list did focus much needed attention on a broader multidimensional notion of personal competence and adaptive behavior. Also, in the section of the 1992 AAMR manual where the theoretical groundwork for the new definition was presented, the importance of describing personal capabilities within a theory of general competence was stressed. McGrew, Bruininks, and Johnson (1996) and Greenspan (1997), however, brought attention to the fact that the actual operational definition and criteria outlined in the 1992 AAMR model was not aligned with any models of personal competence. There was an obvious disconnect between the stated importance of a theoretical model of personal competence and the resultant operational definition and criteria in the 1992 AAMR manual.

The AAMR's most recent definition and classification manual (Luckasson et al., 2002) moves even further toward defining and conceptualizing mental retardation as limitations in the multidimensional construct of personal competence. The 2002 definition is that "mental retardation is a disability characterized by significant limitations both in intellectual functioning and in conceptual, social, and practical adaptive skills. This disability originates before age 18" (p. 1). The authors indicate that intellectual functioning is still best represented by IQ scores when obtained from appropriate assessment instruments and adaptive behavior encompasses the application of conceptual, social, and practical skills to daily life.

Although the 2002 AAMR definition retains the two traditional criteria for diagnosis of mental retardation (i.e., intelligence and adaptive behavior), three different dimensions of personal competence appear to be emerging as the cornerstone of the definition and criteria for diagnosing mental retardation: conceptual intelligence, social intelligence, and practical intelligence. While these terms are not explicitly defined in the 2002 AAMR manual, conceptual intelligence has traditionally referred to abstract intellectual abilities needed to understand symbolic processes (e.g., language) and to master academic or analytic tasks (Greenspan & Granfield, 1992; Greenspan & Driscoll, 1997; McGrew et al., 1996; Schalock, 2002). Skill indicators of conceptual intelligence include receptive and expressive language, reading and writing skills, and mathematical skills (Shalock, 2002). Social intelligence has typically been defined as "a person's ability to understand and to deal effectively with social and interpersonal objects and events" (Greenspan, 1979, p. 483) and includes interpersonal and social skills. Examples of social and interpersonal competency skill indicators are forming and maintaining friendships, participating in group activities, responsibility, and sensitivity and insight (Schalock, 2002). Finally, *practical intelligence* has been described as "the ability to deal with the physical and mechanical aspects of life" (Greenspan, 1979, p. 510) and includes self-maintenance, daily living competencies, vocational activities, and recreational and leisure activities (Greenspan, 1981; Schalock, 2002). Some potential skill indicators of practical intelligence are self-help skills, daily living skills, community living skills, and occupational skills (Schalock, 2002).

The focus on personal competence in the new AAMR definition appears to be more consistent with available models of personal competence than past definitions. Greenspan and Driscoll (1997) recently presented a revised personal competence model comprised of four dimensions: physical competence, affective competence, everyday competence, and academic competence. Each of these domains was further subdivided into eight subdomains. The authors indicate that each of the subdomains could be further broken down into more discrete elements. Thus, the Greenspan and Driscoll model can be considered to be a hierarchical model with several strata.

Measuring Personal Competence

Figure 1 shows an adapted model of personal competence similar to Greenspan's earlier models (Greenspan, 1979, 1981; Greenspan & Granfield, 1992) and is generally consistent with AAMR's 2002 definition and classification system. In addition, this figure reflects a recent attempt to map the theoretical domain of personal competence to the available instruments in the measurement domain (McGrew, 2001). It is important to note that although physical intelligence would not be related to a definition of mental retardation, it would be important to consider it when assessing an individual's overall level of personal competence.[1] If people with mental retardation are to be assessed on the basis of personal competence, it is essential that the field have access to reliable and valid mea-

---

[1]The use of the terms *physical* and *intelligence* in the same phrase may sound unusual but is conceptually similar to Gardner's (1993) notion of bodily–kinesthetic intelligence, which consists of those physical competencies that are probably enhanced in individuals in professions such as dance and sports.

sures of the critical dimensions. Unfortunately, current instrumentation lags behind current need.

As suggested by Thompson et al. (1999), the necessary measurement domain tools required to adequately assess a person's abilities and competencies (as they relate to an evolving definition of mental retardation) may require the use of direct tests that measure traits (e.g., memory)

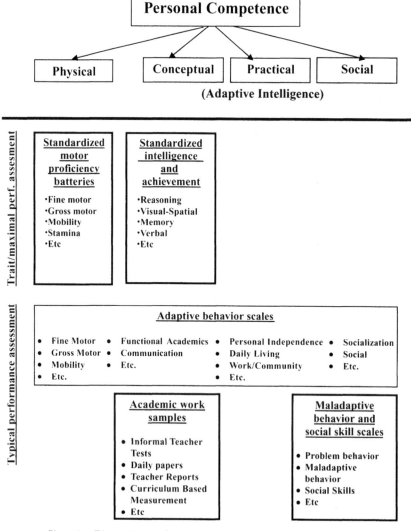

Figure 1. Dimensions and potential measures of personal competence.

under maximal performance conditions as well as indirect and largely third-party checklists or rating skills of typical performance. It is clear in Figure 1 that assessment technology currently exists for directly measuring conceptual intelligence (e.g., Woodcock–Johnson III Battery; Wechsler batteries; standardized achievement batteries). In addition, indicators of typical conceptual performance (e.g., reading performance in the classroom or in an employment setting) can be gleaned from functional academic scales from many current adaptive behavior scales. In addition, informal work samples, curriculum-based measures, and teacher or supervisor reports can provide additional indirect information regarding a person's typical performance in a variety of the conceptual intelligence subdomains.

In the theoretical–measurement domain mapping illustrated in Figure 1, current adaptive behavior scales are considered to provide indications of typical performance across the four major domains of personal competence. This conceptualization recognizes that adaptive behavior, as operationalized by today's scales, does not measure a trait (or set of traits). Rather, adaptive behavior scales provide indirect indicators of typical performance across personal competence domains. Hopefully this recognition will result in improvements in revised and yet-to-be developed measures of adaptive behavior. This recognition also suggests that the field may want to consider dropping the term *adaptive behavior* in favor of a more descriptive term (e.g., typical competence behavior or everyday competence). Similarly, the maladaptive sections of many adaptive behavior scales, as well as available social skills rating scales, can be considered as indicators of typical and atypical social functioning.

The most important information gleaned from Figure 1 is the conclusion that there is a critical lack of reliable and valid instrumentation in the direct/maximal performance domains of practical and social intelligence (McGrew, 2001). Despite decades of attempts to develop direct tests of social intelligence or social awareness, no individually administered and nationally standardized test (or battery of tests) of this construct domain has emerged (Greenspan, 1999a). The practical intelligence direct measurement domain is even less advanced, with serious research in this area currently being in a state of infancy (Wagner, 1994). Recent practical intelligence research on the development of direct measures of *tacit knowledge* (practical domain-specific know-how knowledge) offers some encouragement in this domain (Wagner, 1994).

Clearly, if a personal competence model-driven assessment practice is to realize its potential to improve the identification and classification of people with mental retardation, significant strides must be made in the development of new assessment technology. Direct measures of practical and social intelligence are sorely needed. Possibly, the innovative use of CD-ROM-based standardized vignettes (administered via computer screens) of everyday practical problem-solving and social situations may hold the key to reliable and valid measurement of the constructs of practical and social intelligence. Additionally, as current adaptive scales are revised, and/or as new scales are developed, we encourage those involved to recognize that these scales are not intended to measure a single thing or construct within a person. Rather, items and scales need to be constructed that provide for the best breadth of sampling of a person's typical functioning across physical, conceptual, practical, and social intelligence domains.

From Personal Competence to Support Needs

A major contribution of the 1992 and 2002 AAMR Definition and Classification manuals (Luckasson et al., 1992, 2002) was the emphasis placed on conceptualizing mental retardation as an expression of the interaction between what a person can do and what the environment demands. That is, mental retardation is evidenced when a person's level of *personal competence* does not enable him or her to perform the tasks that his or her environment requires for successful functioning. This interactionist, or *person–environment fit,* orientation provides for a more functional conceptualization of mental retardation than a traditional trait orientation (i.e., mental retardation is a trait within the person). The emphasis on the person–environment interaction leads to a focus on identifying the types of support a person needs to be successful in typical, everyday life settings. Such supports are intended to reduce or eliminate the mismatch between environmental demands and a person's current level of skills. This perspective also assumes that human performance is influenced and can be improved through designing environments that accommodate a diverse range of abilities and needs (e.g., incorporating principles of universal design into the design of buildings, living environments, recreational facilities, and so on) (Steinfeld & Danford, 1999).

A Systematic Approach to Support
Needs Assessment and Planning

Thompson, Hughes, et al. (2002) define supports as "resources and strategies that promote the interests and welfare of individuals and that result in enhanced personal independence and productivity, greater participation in an interdependent society, increased community integration, and/or an improved quality of life" (p. 3). These authors propose a four-component approach for determining support needs and developing plans to meet these needs. The four components are as follows: (a) identifying a person's desired life experiences and goals, (b) determining an individual's intensity of support needs across a wide range of environments and activities, (c) developing an individualized support plan, and (d) monitoring outcomes and assessing the effectiveness of the plan.

To complete the first component, a person-centered planning process (e.g., Butterworth et al., 1993; Mount & Zwernik, 1988) is needed to identify any discrepancies between an individual's current life experiences and conditions and his or her preferred or desired life experiences and conditions. This process involves the consideration of the need to maintain or change a person's life experiences as well as a prioritization of desired outcomes (Thompson, Hughes, et al., 2002).

The second component entails a formal assessment process specifying the general characteristics of a person's support needs. This is accomplished in parallel with or shortly after person-centered planning (i.e., component 1) and should reflect the frequency and duration of specific types of needed supports. Also, a comprehensive assessment of the sources of support that are currently available to a person must be considered. Collectively, this information should provide an adequate and objective set of data from which to identify the intensity of individual support needs and provide guidance for the developing of an Individualized Support Plan (ISP). A scale for measuring an individual's support needs, the Support Intensity Scale (SIS), was recently developed by Thompson, Bryant, et al. (2002). Although the SIS is still in the field test stage of development, results from a preliminary field test of an earlier version of the scale are encouraging (Thompson, Hughes, et al., 2002).

The third component requires the development of an ISP where the sources of support are identified based on a team process that considers resource and service availability or practicality. The fourth component entails follow-up and monitoring of an individual's quality of life and the implementation of the ISP. A key aspect of the fourth component is the planning team's examination of the progress that was made in assisting the individual in realizing the desired conditions and experiences that were specified during person-centered planning. Also, it is important for the planning team to determine whether the conditions and experiences originally specified as priorities should be maintained or revised. Finally, an assessment of the extent to which the ISP was actually implemented is required.

Time will tell whether or not the four-component process described by Thompson, Hughes, et al. (2002) makes a lasting contribution to the assessment and planning of support needs. Support needs is a slippery construct that makes developing specific procedures for systematically identifying the support needs of individuals a challenging task. However, a person–environment fit orientation to mental retardation renders the need for support the definitive characteristic of persons with mental retardation. Therefore, it is imperative that efforts to develop reliable measures of support needs are undertaken.

Conclusion

Historical attempts to define mental retardation have typically emphasized important aspects of personal and social competence and aspects of the environment (cf. Davies, 1959; Scheerenberger, 1983). While these emphases in definitions of intellectual disability have drawn criticism, even a casual review of research during the past 100 years attests to the powerful influence of these constructs on defining, understanding, and supporting persons with mental retardation. The continuing development and refinement of measurement, the refinement of conceptual models of development and adaptation, and the advancement of statistical modeling are leading to the conclusion that personal competence and features of environment play a profound role in identifying people with mental retardation and in providing them with necessary support.

The seminal contributions of Itard, Seguin, Montessori, and Doll on the important role of personal competence and the role of environmental influences in human adaptation and performance are still timely in contemporary efforts to define mental retardation and other developmental disabilities. We feel it is critically important to explore and define the many features of personal competence and the critical features of environment that limit or enhance aspects of human adaptation and performance.

There is ample and growing evidence that the historic emphasis upon personal competency and adaptation is critical in defining mental retardation. With this emphasis, it is likely that we will witness continuingly more sophisticated measures, with greater technical soundness, in assessing aspects of performance outside more standard cognitive and academic achievement measures. Similar energy should be expended to improve assessment of the role of environment in influencing behavior and development and in enhancing human performance.

Today there is a better understanding of the various pieces of the puzzle than in the past. Despite all of the consternation and debate over various definitions of mental retardation during the past decade, we are optimistic about the future. Progress in measuring essential dimensions of mental retardation will yield progress in supporting the population of persons with mental retardation in a thoughtful and equitable manner. There is no better time to complete the work that is needed to gain a better understanding of each piece of the puzzle and an improved appreciation of how each of these pieces fit together to create greater opportunity for persons with intellectual disabilities.

References

Ad Hoc Committee on Terminology and Classification. (2001). Request for comments on proposed new edition of mental retardation: Definition, classification, and systems of supports. *AAMR News and Notes, 14*(5), 1, 9–12.

Baumeister, A. A., Kupstas, F. D., & Woodley-Zanthos, P. (1993). *The new morbidity: Recommendations for action and an updated guide to state planning for the preventions of mental retardation and related conditions associated with socioeconomic conditions.* Washington, DC: President's Committee on Mental Retardation.

Bruininks, R. H., McGrew, K. S., & Maruyama, G. (1988). Structure of adaptive behavior in samples with and without mental retardation. *American Journal on Mental Retardation, 93*, 265–272.

Bruininks, R. H., Thurlow, M., & Gilman, C. J. (1987). Adaptive behavior and mental retardation. *Journal of Special Education, 21*, 69–88.

Butterworth, J., Hagner, D., Heikkinen, B., Faris, S., DeMello, S., & McDonough, K. (1993). *Whole life planning: A guide for organizers and facilitators.* Boston: Children's Hospital, Institute for Community Inclusion.

Clausen, J. (1972). The continuing problem of defining mental deficiency. *Journal of Special Education, 6*, 97–106.

Coulter, W. A., & Morrow, H. W. (1978). A contemporary conception of adaptive behavior within the scope of psychological assessment. In W. A. Coulter & H. W. Morrow (Eds.), *Adaptive behavior: Concepts and measurements* (pp. 3–20). New York: Grune & Stratton.

Danforth, S. (1997). On what basis hope? Modern progress and postmodern possibilities. *Mental Retardation, 35*, 93–106.

Davies, S. P. (1959). *The mentally retarded in society.* New York: Columbia University Press.

Doll, E. A. (1936). President's address. *Journal of Psycho-Asthetics, 18*, 40–41.

Doll, E. A. (1941). The essentials of an inclusive concept of mental deficiency. *American Journal of Mental Deficiency, 46*, 214–219.

Gardner, H. (1993). *Frames of mind: The theory of multiple intelligences.* New York: Basic Books.

Greenspan, S. (1979). Social intelligence in the retarded. In N. R. Ellis (Ed.), *Handbook of mental deficiency: Psychological theory and research* (2nd ed., pp. 483–532). Hillsdale, NJ: Lawrence Erlbaum Associates, Inc.

Greenspan, S. (1981). Defining childhood social competence: A proposed working model. In B. K. Keough (Ed.), *Advances in special education, Vol. 3. Socialization influences on exceptionality* (pp. 1–29). Greenwich, CT: JAI.

Greenspan, S. (1997). Dead manual walking? Why the 1992 AAMR definition needs redoing. *Education and Training in Mental Retardation and Developmental Disabilities, 32*, 179–190.

Greenspan, S. (1999a). A contextualist perspective on adaptive behavior. In R. L. Schalock (Ed.), *Adaptive behavior and its measurement: Implications for the field of mental retardation* (pp.15–42). Washington, DC: American Association on Mental Retardation.

Greenspan, S. (1999b). What is meant by mental retardation? *International Review of Psychiatry, 11,* 6–18.

Greenspan, S., & Driscoll, J. (1997). The role of intelligence in a broad model of personal competence. In D. P. Flanagan, J. L. Genshaft, and P. L. Harrison (Eds.), *Contemporary intellectual assessment: Theories, tests, and issues* (pp. 131–150). New York: Guilford.

Greenspan, S., & Granfield, J. M. (1992). Reconsidering the construct of mental retardation: Implications of a model of social competence. *American Journal on Mental Retardation, 96,* 442–453.

Heber, R. (1959). A manual on terminology and classification in mental retardation. *Monograph Supplement to the American Journal of Mental Deficiency, 62.*

Hockenbury, J. C., Kauffman, J. M., & Hallahan, D. P. (1999–2000). What is right about special education? *Exceptionality, 8,* 3–11.

Jacobson, J. W., & Mulick, J. A. (1992). A new definition of mentally retarded or a new definition of practice. *Psychology in Mental Retardation and Developmental Disabilities, 18,* 9–14.

Kauffman, J. M. (1999). Commentary: Today's special education and its messages for tomorrow. *The Journal of Special Education, 32,* 244–254.

Kliewer, C., & Biklen, D. (1996). Labeling: Who wants to be called retarded? In W. Stainback and S. Stainback (Eds.), *Controversial issues confronting special education: Divergent perspectives* (pp. 83–95). Boston: Allyn & Bacon.

Lewis, D. R., Bruininks, R. H., Thurlow, M. L., & McGrew, K. (1989). A note on the use of earnings functions and human capital theory in assessing special education. *Economics of Education Review, 8,* 285–290.

Luckasson, R., Borthwick-Duffy, S., Buntinx, W. H. E., Coulter, D. L., Craig, E. M., Reeve, A., et al. (2002). *Mental retardation: Definition, classification, and systems of support* (10th ed.). Washington, DC: American Association on Mental Retardation.

Luckasson, R., Coulter, D. L., Polloway, E. A., Reiss, S., Schalock, R. L., Snell, M. E., et al. (1992). *Mental retardation: Definition, classification, and systems of support* (9th ed.). Washington, DC: American Association on Mental Retardation.

MacMillan, D. L., Gresham, F. M., & Siperstein, G. N. (1993). Conceptual and psychometric concerns about the 1992 AAMR definitions of mental retardation. *American Journal of Mental Retardation, 98,* 325–335.

Matson, J. L., Epstein, M. H., & Cullinan, D. (1984). A factor analytic study of the Quay–Peterson Scale with mentally retarded adolescents. *Education and Training of the Mentally Retarded, 19,* 150–154.

McGrew, K. S. (2001, October). *The big picture of assessment: The Forrest Gump model.* Presentation at the Wisconsin School Psychologists Association Annual Conference, Manitowoc, WI.

McGrew, K. S., & Bruininks, R. H. (1989). The factor structure of adaptive behavior. *School Psychology Review, 18,* 64–81.

McGrew, K. S., Bruininks, R. H., & Johnson, D. R. (1996). A confirmatory factor analysis investigation of Greenspan's model of personal competence. *American Journal on Mental Retardation, 100,* 533–545.

Meyers, C., Nihira, K., & Zetlin, A. (1979). The measurement of adaptive behavior. In N. R. Ellis (Ed.), *Handbook on mental deficiency: Psychological theory and research* (2nd ed., pp. 431–481). Hillsdale, NJ: Lawrence Erlbaum Associates, Inc.

Mount, B., & Zwernik, K. (1988). *It's never too early, it's never too late: A booklet about personal futures planning.* Mears Park Centre, MN: Metropolitan Council.

Nihira, K. (1999). Adaptive behavior: A historical overview. In R. L. Schalock (Ed.), *Adaptive behavior and its measurement: Implications for the field of mental retardation* (pp. 15–42). Washington, DC: American Association on Mental Retardation.

Owens, E. P., & Bowling, D. H. (1970). Internal consistency and factor structure of the Preschool Attainment Record. *American Journal of Mental Deficiency, 75,* 170–171.

Schalock, R. L. (2002). Mental retardation: A condition characterized by significant limitations in practical, conceptual, and social skills. Manuscript submitted for publication.

Scheerenberger, R. (1983). *A history of mental retardation.* Baltimore: Brookes.

Smith, J. D. (1998). Defining mental retardation: The natural history of a concept. In A. Hilton & R. Ringlaben (Eds.), *Best and promising practices in developmental disabilities* (pp. 15–21). Austin, TX: PRO-ED.

Sparrow, S. S., & Cicchetti, D. V. (1978). Behavior rating inventory for moderately, severely, and profoundly retarded persons. *American Journal of Mental Deficiency, 82,* 365–374.

Steinfeld, E., & Danford, G. S. (Eds). (1999). *Enabling environments: Measuring the impact of environment on disability and rehabilitation.* New York: Kluwer Academic/Plenum.

Thompson, J. R., McGrew, K. S. & Bruininks, R. H. (1999). Adaptive and maladaptive behavior: Functional and structural characteristics. In R. L. Schalock (Ed.), *Adaptive behavior and its measurement: Implications for the field of mental retardation* (pp. 15–42). Washington, DC: American Association on Mental Retardation.

Thompson, J. R., Bryant, B., Campbell, E. M., Craig, E. M., Hughes, C., Rotholtz, D. A., et al. (2002). Support Intensity Scale. Unpublished assessment scale.

Thompson, J. R., Hughes, C., Schalock, R. L., Silverman, W., Tassé, M. J., Bryant. B., et al. (2002). Integrating supports in assessment and planning. *Mental Retardation, 40,* 390–405.

Tredgold, A. F. (1922). *Mental deficiency.* New York: Wood.

Wagner, R. K. (1994). Practical intelligence. In R. J. Sternberg (Ed.), *The encyclopedia of human intelligence* (pp. 821–828). New York: Macmillan.

Widaman, K. F., Borthwick-Duffy, S. A., & Little, T. D. (1991). The structure and development of adaptive behaviors. In N. W. Bray (Ed.), *International review of research in mental retardation, 17,* 1–54.

Widaman, K. F., & McGrew, K. S. (1996). The structure of adaptive behavior. In J. W. Jacobson & J. A. Mulick (Eds.), *Manual of diagnosis and professional practice in mental retardation* (pp. 97–110). Washington, DC: American Psychological Association.

Ysseldyke, J. E., Algozzine, B., & Thurlow, M. L. (1992). *Critical issues in special education.* Boston: Houghton Mifflin.

Zigler, E., Balla, D., & Hodapp, R. (1984). On the definition and classification of mental retardation. *American Journal of Mental Deficiency, 89,* 215–230.

PEABODY JOURNAL OF EDUCATION, 77(2), 40–63
Copyright © 2002, Lawrence Erlbaum Associates, Inc.

Applications and Challenges in Dynamic Assessment

H. Carl Haywood
Peabody College
Vanderbilt University

David Tzuriel
School of Education
Bar Ilan University

Dynamic assessment is described as a subset of interactive assessment that includes deliberate and planned mediational teaching and the assessment of the effects of that teaching on subsequent performance. Its historical roots are traced to Vygotsky and Feuerstein and rests on four assumptions: (a) Accumulated knowledge is not the best indication of ability to acquire new knowledge. (b) Everyone functions at less than 100% of capacity. (c) The best test of any performance is a sample of that performance. (d) There are many obstacles that can mask one's ability; when the obstacles are removed, greater ability than was suspected is often revealed. The authors review what is known so far about dynamic assessment and give examples of its utility as a tool for research and clinical work in psychopathology, neuropsychology, education, the study of cultural differences, and developmental research. Some persistent problems are noted as well.

Dynamic Assessment

Some Concepts and a Little History

Traditional (static, normative) methods of psychological and psychoeducational assessment do not require or permit active intervention on the

Requests for reprints should be sent to H. Carl Haywood, 144 Brighton Close, Nashville, TN 37205.

part of examiners. In general, methods in which the role of examiners is more active and intervening are frequently referred to as *interactive assessment*. One subclass of interactive assessment includes those methods in which the activity and intervention of examiners is specifically designed to produce at least a temporary change in the cognitive functioning of examinees—a subclass known as *dynamic assessment* (DA). The term *dynamic* implies change. A major goal is to assess processes of thinking that are themselves constantly changing (hence the term *assessment* rather than *measurement*). In addition, examiners do some active and directed teaching precisely in order to produce change. Thus, the basic datum in DA is a change variable: How do examinees learn new things? How does the removal of learning obstacles change their performance? (See, e.g., Haywood, 1992, 1997; Haywood & Tzuriel, 1992.) According to this approach, DA refers to assessment of thinking, perception, learning, and problem solving by an active teaching process aimed at modifying cognitive functioning. The contrasting approach, static testing, is testing in which examiners present problems or questions to examinees and record their responses with no attempt to intervene in order to change, guide, or improve the examinees' performance.

Although the concept of DA is not new, it is not yet widely practiced and is still virtually unknown to many psychologists and educators (see, e.g., Elliott, 1993; Lidz, 1992; Tzuriel, 2000b, 2001, 2002). There are many reasons for this state of affairs—some conceptual and others quite practical. We discuss the obstacles to the widespread use of DA at the end of this article.

As applied to the assessment of individual differences in ability, especially learning ability, the basic ideas underlying DA are deceptively simple:

- Accumulated knowledge is not the best indication of one's ability to acquire new knowledge, although the two are highly correlated.
- Everybody functions at considerably less than 100% of full capacity; therefore, everybody can do better (see, e.g., Vygotsky, 1978).
- The best test of any performance is a sample of that performance itself (e.g., Cronbach, 1970; Freeman, 1950); therefore, assessment of learning abilities can be accomplished effectively with the use of learning tasks, especially those involving teaching—a condition that characterizes school learning.
- There are identifiable obstacles to one's access to and effective application of one's intelligence. Such obstacles include ignorance; impulsivity; impoverished vocabulary; cultural differences in learning habits, styles, and attitudes; poor self-concept as learners; and a host of motivational variables; plus, of course, inadequate development of important cognitive

and metacognitive structures and strategies. By removing some of those obstacles, one can reveal the ability to function more adequately.

What this last assumption is saying is that there are many factors that can mask one's intelligence (Haywood, Tzuriel, & Vaught, 1992). An important corollary is that those masking variables are not uniform but may differ markedly from person to person.

The idea of actually intervening in testing situations in order to discover what examinees would be able to do with some help seems to have been introduced by Vygotsky (1986/1934). Vygotsky first described the process in the following way:

> Most of the psychological investigations concerned with school learning measured the level of mental development of the child by making him solve certain standardized problems. The problems he was able to solve by himself were supposed to indicate the level of his mental development at the particular time. But in this way, only the completed part of the child's development can be measured, which is far from the whole story. We tried a different approach. Having found that the mental age of two children was, let us say, eight, we gave each of them harder problems than he could manage on his own and provided some slight assistance: the first step in a solution, a leading question, or some other form of help. We discovered that one child could, in cooperation, solve problems designed for twelve-year-olds, while the other could not go beyond problems intended for nine-year-olds. The discrepancy between a child's actual mental age and the level he reaches in solving problems with assistance indicates the zone of his proximal development; in our example, this zone is four for the first child and one for the second. Can we truly say that their mental development is the same? Experience has shown that the child with the larger *zone of proximal development* (ZPD) will do much better in school. This measure gives a more helpful clue than mental age does to the dynamics of intellectual progress. (pp. 186–187)

Vygotsky believed that his interventional testing method opened a developmental window on the future, showing psychologists what would happen in the next phases of a child's development. As it has turned out, this is not exactly true; rather, it provides a view of what could happen in subsequent development, provided that children have opportunities to receive certain kinds of cognitive developmental assistance. In other words, Vygotsky's method yielded optimistic estimates of children's learning potential, but those optimistic predictions were doomed to failure if nothing were done to assist in the realization of the unmasked potential. That is precisely the situation we face all too frequently today: children throughout the world whose learning potential is first underestimated and then not developed, inviting the underestimation to be true.

As is true of most important ideas, there were certainly intimations of a need for something like DA prior to Vygotsky's writing. Wolfgang Köhler (1917), reporting on testing the intelligence of the great apes, wrote,

> If it is no longer essential to investigate how the chimpanzee can act intelligently without help, it can be ascertained in further tests to what extent he can learn to understand functionally complex structures (and situations) if he is given all possible help. (p. 131, cited by Guthke, 1992, p. 214)

Alfred Binet (1911), after observing pupils with mental retardation in Paris schools, stated that the time the teachers were spending trying to teach the academic content of the early grades might better be spent helping the children first acquire more adequate tools of learning (Haywood & Paour, 1992), thereby implying that the failure to develop such learning tools constitutes an unnecessary obstacle to better learning. His suggestion was a precursor of what later became cognitive education, but it also led Binet to propose that attention be given to assessment of the processes of learning rather than exclusively to the products of prior opportunities to learn (Binet, 1911). In spite of his enthusiasm for this idea, Binet did little to pursue it. Similarly, André Rey (1934) wrote about assessment of learning processes in situations that involved teaching, but then continued, over the next 30 years, to develop normative, standardized tests of already-acquired knowledge and skill. Although these and other investigators suggested measurement of the ability to learn as part of intelligence and as an ideal method for testing mental abilities, the interest in, elaboration, and spread of the concept of DA occurred only in the 1970s with the introduction of Vygotsky's theory by Brown and Ferrara (1985), and Feuerstein's ideas (Haywood, 1977a, 1977b) to the wider psychological world.

Even today, there are very few systematic DA programs that have demonstrated satisfactory metric characteristics. We discuss some measurement issues toward the end of this article.

What Is Known So Far

In spite of the lamentable paucity of empirical research on DA itself, it is possible to extract some reliable conclusions from that small body of studies. Some of these conclusions are presented and discussed in the following paragraphs.

Test performance improves after teaching or mediation. This conclusion is shared by almost everyone who has done research on DA. The magnitude of such improvement in performance may depend on the kind of teaching, its intensity, the specific nature of each person's cognitive barriers, and the psychological distance between the content of the teaching and the content of the performance tests (see, e.g., Budoff, 1987; Carlson & Wiedl, 1992; Feuerstein, Rand, & Hoffman, 1979; Gordon & Haywood, 1969; Guthke, 1992; Guthke & Wingenfeld, 1992; Haywood, Filler, Shifman, & Chatelanat, 1975; Tzuriel, 2001; Tzuriel & Haywood, 1992).

Mediation of logic strategies leads to greater performance improvement. As compared to mediation of logic strategies, mere teaching of content or giving hints to the correct answers does not lead to greater performance improvement. Some researchers have systematically compared the relative effectiveness of different intervening activities, including mediation of logic structures, *graduated prompts,* and no intervening activity between pretests and posttests. Invariably, mediation leads to greater performance gains than no intervention as well as to greater gains than graduated prompting (see, e.g., Burns, 1991; Kester & Peña, 2001; Missiuna & Samuels, 1989).

Mediated strategies and the solving of new problems. In many, but not all, DA studies, it is possible to transfer mediated strategies to the solving of new problems. This is, of course, the heart of the matter. If all one does is to produce higher test scores, without transfer of the mediated cognitive and metacognitive operations and strategies to content areas well beyond those involved in the mediational teaching, such an achievement is quite modest. That demonstration is not entirely worthless because one does not do what one cannot do; therefore, reaching a higher level of performance is indeed evidence that one is capable of doing that. The problem, again, is that without transfer, it is quite possible that the conditions that produced the improved performance may never come about again, so one is left with an empty prediction of higher abilities than will ever be demonstrated. The typical finding on transfer of mediated concepts, operations, and strategies in DA is that near transfer is easily obtained, whereas far transfer is demonstrated when the mediational teaching contains pedagogical strategies deliberately designed to promote transfer. In other words, transfer is not an accident and does not occur by chance but must be promoted in direct and active ways (see, e.g., Burns, 1991; Paour, 1992; Paour & Soavi, 1992.)

Estimates of learning potential.   Estimates of learning potential gained from DA are often more substantially related to subsequent learning and performance in teaching situations, such as in school, than are estimates of intelligence gained from static, normative testing. One might well ask : Why are we even interested in such a phenomenon, given that most DA advocates are less concerned with the prediction of group performance than they are with learning how to defeat pessimistic predictions made for individuals on the basis of static testing? One answer lies in that very distinction between group and individual prediction. Static, normative tests of intelligence do a superb job of forecasting the future performance, especially the academic achievement, of large groups, although the predictive correlation usually does not exceed +.70 or +.75, leaving a substantial portion of the variance in achievement scores statistically unassociated with scores on the predictor tests. DA is often especially interested in that portion of the remaining variance that is not attributable to the unreliability of the predictor tests, the unreliability of the criterion tests, or their joint unreliability. That residue is likely to constitute a validity problem: Future learning is not perfectly predicted by knowing how much has already been learned, especially given unequal opportunities to learn. (For evidence on this major point, see Budoff, 1987; Guthke, 1992; and Tzuriel, 1992a.) Proponents of DA are also typically more concerned about individual performance than about the performance of groups.

Observations of DA and static, normative testing.   Teachers gain more useful information for their teaching from observing DA than from observing static, normative testing. Nobody whose work we have read in the last generation has actually maintained that intelligence test scores help teachers to select content and teaching strategies. It is certainly true that some teachers have used low IQ as an excuse for not trying very hard to teach children ("we know they can't learn, so why frustrate them by insisting that they do what they cannot do?"); indeed, very high IQ is also sometimes used as such an excuse ("they'll learn it no matter what I do"). In several studies, teachers have been given information derived from static testing or DA and have then been asked to indicate how much they learned and how much they were helped by each. The difference is typically, and positively, in favor of DA. The difference is even more dramatic when teachers actually observe the two situations, rather than merely reading reports based on those assessment strategies. Of course, one would like to see less reliance on self-report in the criterion variable in favor of actual observation of what teachers do in their classrooms rather than what they say has been important to them (see, e.g., Delclos, Vye, Burns, Bransford, & Hasselbring, 1992; Benjamin & Lomofsky, 2002; and Vye, Burns, Delclos, & Bransford, 1987).

Obtainable knowledge. As a research tool, DA can yield knowledge that would be unobtainable, or would be much more difficult to obtain, from static, normative testing. This is especially true when one is faced with examinees who are reluctant to respond to questions, whose language facility is seriously impaired, or whose psychopathology blocks their ability or inclination to engage in problem-solving tasks effectively. Less obvious and dramatic circumstances, but ones that occur far more frequently, include *transculturality* (i.e., transplantation to a quite different cultural milieu), social discrimination (often associated with transculturality), an inadequate knowledge base relative to one's age, negative self-concept as a learner, and unproductive habits when faced with problem-solving requirements. In the following sections of this article, we discuss in greater detail some research in which DA was an essential and valuable tool for information gathering and interpretation (see, e.g., Haywood & Wingenfeld, 1992), as well as developmental research in which DA data (as indicative of cognitive modifiability) were predicted by mother–child interactions, and evaluation of cognitive education programs.

Potential is a useful concept for habilitation or rehabilitation efforts. For example, in the diagnostic study and cognitive redevelopment of persons who have sustained brain injuries (Haywood & Miller, 2002; Heinrich, 1991) and in the search for rehabilitative approaches for persons with major psychiatric disorders (e.g., Sclan, 1986), DA has been an indispensable research tool.

Defeating the pessimistic predictions from static tests. Even when static, normative test scores are shown to be better predictors of subsequent academic achievement than performance on DA tasks, it is the information gained from DA that informs us about how to defeat the pessimistic predictions from static tests. We do not assert that static, normative tests of intelligence are biased, or wrong, or that they themselves discriminate against subgroups in our population (Gutkin & Reynolds, 1980; Jensen, 1980, 1985; Utley, Haywood, & Masters, 1992). The point here is that pessimistic predictions derived from standardized intelligence tests are disastrously likely to come true! The far more important question is how to defeat those predictions (Haywood, 1997). In order to respond to that kind of question, one must examine the combination of research on DA and research on cognitive education—or, in the latter case, on any educational or psychological intervention designed to enhance the educability of children and youth.

Using Dynamic Assessment to Get at Elusive Knowledge

We referred earlier to the ability of DA to yield information that is difficult or impossible to acquire by other known methods, especially in certain clinical populations. In this section we discuss some studies that demonstrate that point, not attempting to be exhaustive but merely illustrative (see also Haywood & Wingenfeld, 1992).

Research in Psychopathology

Schizophrenia has generally been described as primarily a thought disorder, although its more florid manifestations include perceptual disorders as well. Sclan (1986) used DA to examine cognitive processes in psychiatric patients with schizophrenia. He gave two instruments, the Representational Stencil Design Test (RSDT; Feuerstein et al., 1979; Feuerstein, Haywood, Rand, Hoffman, & Jensen, 1986) and the Test of Verbal Abstracting (TVA; Haywood, 1986) to 30 hospitalized patients with paranoid and nonparanoid schizophrenia. As usual in DA, participants were given a pretest in a static mode (no help), then mediation of cognitive concepts and metacognitive strategies related to these tasks, and finally a posttest, again in a static mode. Nonparanoid patients made significantly more errors than did paranoid patients on 6 of 8 possible error types on both tasks. A more important and relevant finding was that the paranoid patients derived greater benefit from the interpolated mediation than did the nonparanoid patients; that is, they made greater gains from pretest to posttest, presumably as a function of the interpolated mediation. Further, the paranoid patients made their large differential gains principally with respect to reduction of errors on items that required more sophisticated abstract cognitive processes; that is, the more cognitively complex and difficult the task, the greater the benefit that the paranoid (but not the nonparanoid) patients derived from cognitive and metacognitive mediation. By intervening within the test, Sclan discovered the relatively more responsive nature of the logic processes of paranoid schizophrenic patients.

Research in Neuropsychology

Heinrich (1991) investigated the ability of patients with closed head injuries to improve their psychological test performance as a function of the interpolated mediation that is part of DA. His principal instrument was the Halstead Category Test (Reitan & Wolfson, 1985), with the posttest version of this test serving as a near-transfer task and the Concept Formation subtest of the Woodcock–Johnson Psycho-Educational Assessment Battery (Woodcock & Johnson, 1977) serving as a far-transfer task. He examined 22 patients divided into two groups: experimental (with interpolated mediation) and control (without mediation). He found that the interpolated mediation was associated with significantly higher scores on the near-transfer task, but comparison on the far-transfer task, although appearing to favor mediation, was not statistically significant. As Haywood and Wingenfeld (1992) reported,

> Mediation reduced the variance in the near-transfer scores (and) also significantly decreased the correlations of the pretest with both the near-transfer and the far-transfer posttests, suggesting that mediation of cognitive processes had interacted with individual differences in the subjects' initial rank order on these tasks; that is, they responded differentially to mediation. (p. 257)

In contrast to expectations based on clinical lore, the brain-injured patients who were given interpolated mediation demonstrated an ability to learn conceptual tasks, suggesting that the potential for cognitive rehabilitation may be greater than had been thought possible.

In a more recent study, Haywood and Miller (2002) used group-administered DA procedures to study the potential for cognitive change in adults who had sustained traumatic brain injuries. They gave Haywood's (1986) TVA plus an associated Verbal Memory Test (Miller, 2002), the Complex Figure test (Osterrieth, 1944; Rey, 1941, 1959) and Feuerstein's (Feuerstein et al., 1979, 1986) RSDT to brain-injured adults in a test–teach–test paradigm. Analyses indicated that (a) group administration of DA procedures is both possible and useful with adults with traumatic brain injuries; (b) the participants made significant improvement in test performance following interpolated mediation; (c) the most dramatic improvement came on the most cognitively complex task, the RSDT (see

Sclan's study); and, (d) the experience of having mediation of important cognitive concepts and metacognitive strategies led to significant improvement in memory performances, both on the Complex Figure and on the Verbal Memory Test, the latter not having been specifically mediated at all. This study suggested, again, the potential for cognitive redevelopment in persons with traumatic brain injuries.

Applications in Education

Previous research has shown generally that standardized intelligence test scores underestimate the abilities of children who come from low socioeconomic levels or who have learning difficulties (e.g., Hamers, Hessels, & van Luit, 1991; Hessels, 1997; Resing, 1997; Tzuriel, 1989, 2000a, 2000b, 2001; Tzuriel & Klein, 1985). Tzuriel and Klein (1985) used the Children's Analogical Thinking Modifiability (CATM) test with four groups: (a) socioeconomically disadvantaged children, (b) socioeconomically advantaged children, (c) children with special educational needs, and (d) mental-age matched children with mental retardation. The highest pre- to postteaching gains were found among the disadvantaged and advantaged groups, whereas the other groups showed small and insignificant gains. A group of children with mental retardation (older children with a mental age equal to kindergarten level), however, showed significant improvement when a partial credit scoring method was applied (i.e., some credit given for each correctly solved dimension of the test: color, size, and shape). This last finding indicates that the children with retardation have difficulty integrating all sources of information and therefore showed gains only according to the partial credit method.

In another study higher pre- to postteaching gains were found among socioeconomically disadvantaged than among advantaged students (Tzuriel, 1989). Similarly, disadvantaged kindergarten children showed initially lower performance than did advantaged children, but they improved their performance significantly on the Children's Seriational Thinking Modifiability (CSTM) test (Tzuriel, 1995) from the pre- to postteaching phase and narrowed the gap with the advantaged group. This result is interpreted as an indication of the relatively higher cognitive potential of the low-functioning children than is expected based on the preteaching score (i.e., static test). Tzuriel (1989) recognized the fact that the frequently found higher pre- to postteaching gains of the low- over the high-functioning children might also be attributed to a ceiling effect in high-functioning children, but the magnitude of gains clearly indicates that mediation is more effective with children who have a lower initial performance level. There is inherent in such observations the question of regression to the mean: Would low-functioning children be expected to perform at a higher level, and high-functioning children at a lower level, on subsequent administrations of the tasks? That possibility is answered, to some extent, by the use of nonmediated control conditions, that is, similar participants who do not receive mediation.

Comparison of performance on static tests and DA tasks has typically revealed higher levels of functioning on DA than on static tests. For example, Tzuriel and Klein (1985) reported that performance, relative to test norms, on the CATM was higher than on Raven's Colored Progressive Matrices (RCPM; Raven, 1956) given as a static test. The differences were clearer when the analogical items of the RCPM were compared to the CATM problems. For example, the advantaged and disadvantaged children scored 69% and 64% on the CATM, respectively, as compared to 39% and 44% on the RCPM, respectively. Performances on the Children's Inferential Thinking Modifiability test (CITM; Tzuriel, 1989, 1992b) with 5- and 6-year-old kindergarten children ($n = 223$) revealed that in some of the items the pre- to postteaching improvement was about 50%. Our argument, which is based on theory, clinical experience, and extensive research, is that the postteaching performance reflects children's abilities much more accurately than does preteaching performance.

The effects of teaching on improvement of performance has been revealed more clearly in difficult tasks than in easy tasks (Tzuriel, 1989, 1995; see previous discussion of studies in neuropsychology). This result verifies what is known clinically, that mediation is most effective, and most needed, in complex and/or abstract tasks. These findings support results of many studies, using a variety of DA tasks, showing significant positive correlations between difficulty level of items and level of improvement on these items (Tzuriel, 1997, 2001).

These studies, conducted in educational settings, not only suggest that children from socioeconomically disadvantaged circumstances and those with special educational needs frequently have more potential ability than is estimated by standardized intelligence tests, but they also point to some useful classroom strategies for teaching such children. Among such useful strategies, derived from the mediation that appeared to produce better performance, would be (a) clear specification of the tasks with which the children are presented, (b) refusal to accept ignorance as an indicator of inability, (c) mediation of essential metacognitive operations within learning tasks, (d) special attention to affective/motivational barriers to investment in learning, and (e) expectation of success.

Applications in Assessment of Cultural Differences

DA has been found to be useful in comparing groups from different cultural backgrounds (Guthke & Al-Zoubi, 1987; Hessels & Hamers, 1993; Kaniel, Tzuriel, Feuerstein, Ben-Shachar, & Eitan, 1991; Skuy & Shmukler, 1987; Tzuriel & Kaufman, 1999). In general, culturally different children perform much better in DA than in static tests. For example, Tzuriel and Kaufman (1999) compared children from two distinctively different cultures, Israeli and Ethiopian. A major question raised recently with Ethiopian immigrants to Israel is how to assess their learning potential, in view of the fact that their scores on static intelligence tests are low and that standard testing procedures inaccurately reflect these children's abilities. The Ethiopian immigrants had to overcome a civilization gap in order to adapt to Israeli society. This issue transcends the specific context of the Ethiopian immigrants, both theoretically and pragmatically. The main hypothesis of the investigators was that many of these immigrants would reveal cultural differences but not cultural deprivation; therefore, they would reveal high levels of modifiability within a DA situation. The Ethiopian group was compared to a group of Israeli-born children on the RCPM (static) and on two young children's DA measures: the CATM and the CITM. The findings showed initial superiority on all tests of the Israeli-born comparison group over the Ethiopian group. The Ethiopian children's scores were lower than those of the Israeli-born children on the preteaching phase of both DA tests, but they improved their performance more than the Israeli children did and narrowed the gap in the post-teaching performance. The gap between the two groups was even narrower in a transfer phase involving more difficult problems. In spite of the initial superiority of the Israeli-born children in every test, after a short but intensive teaching process, the Ethiopian group narrowed the gap significantly.

The difference between the two groups in the free-recall subtest of the CITM (children are asked to recall from memory the objects used in the previous phases of the test) was very small and nonsignificant. The good performance of the Ethiopian children on this task probably reflects the Ethiopian culture of oral learning and rote learning strategies. Support for this interpretation was found in the correlation between the CITM–free-recall task and the RCPM: free-recall was significantly correlated with the RCPM score only in the Ethiopian group (Fisher's $z = 2.89$; $p < .01$). This result was explained by the Ethiopian children's tendency to use similar cognitive processes in solving both tasks, as compared to the Israeli-born children's tendency to apply different processes.

One of the most impressive results was found with the classification subtest of the CITM. The children are asked to classify the pictures they have been exposed to with the inferential problems. After the preteaching phase, the child is given a teaching phase in which a short (1–2 min) mediation is given on some principles of classification. This is followed by a parallel postteaching phase in which each of the pre- and postteaching phases has a maximal score of 12. The Ethiopian group showed much higher improvement (from .70 to 9.00), as compared to the Israeli-born group (10.20 to 12.00). The investigators explained the very low initial performance of the Ethiopian children as lack of familiarity with classification tasks rather than lack of ability. These results coincide with cross-cultural research findings indicating that individuals in many non-Western nations classify items into functional rather than into taxonomic categories (i.e., Luria, 1976; Scribner, 1984; Sharpe, Cole, & Lave, 1979). These data are clearly open to interpretation as regression effects, especially given that the Israeli children were near the test ceiling at preteaching and actually at the ceiling at postteaching. Nevertheless, the demonstration that the Ethiopian children were capable of improved performance given minimal mediational intervention bears its own weight.

The pre- to postteaching improvements of the Ethiopian kindergarten group are similar to those reported previously on older Ethiopian children (Kaniel et al., 1991) and to findings in other countries showing smaller differences between minority and mainstream groups after rather than before a mediation given within a DA process (Guthke & Al-Zoubi, 1987; Hessels & Hamers, 1993; Skuy & Shmukler, 1987).

Use of DA in Developmental Research

The account of developmental research using DA is based on 10 studies, carried out at Bar Ilan University, in which parent–child mediated learning strategies were observed in relation to children's cognitive modifiability. Tzuriel has reviewed the findings in detail (1999, 2001). Two topics from this series are discussed in this article: (a) prediction of children's cognitive modifiability by mother–child strategies of mediated learning and (b) the relative prediction of cognitive modifiability by *distal* (mother's socioeconmic status (SES), mother's IQ, mother's emotional attitudes toward the child, child's personality orientation, the amount of time parents spend with their children during the week) and *proximal* (mediated learning interaction) variables.

In almost all of the studies, children's postteaching scores on DA measures were better predicted by mother–child interactions involving mediated learning experiences (MLEs) than by static test scores or preteaching scores of DA measures. In one of the first studies (Tzuriel & Eran, 1990), a sample of kibbutz mother–child dyads ($n = 47$) were observed in a free play situation for 20 min. The young children (22 boys and 25 girls, age range = 4.7 to 7.8 years) were then given the RCPM (Raven, 1956) and the CITM tests. Three stepwise regression analyses were carried out, with the RCPM and MLE total scores assigned as predictors of either the CITM preteaching, CITM postteaching, or CITM gain score. The CITM preteaching (static) score was predicted only by the RCPM ($R = .40; p < .004$), the CITM postteaching was predicted by both MLE total and RCPM ($R = .69; p < .002$), and the CITM gain was predicted only by the MLE total score ($R = .43; p < .001$). The pattern of prediction across the three analyses showed a gradual increase in the predicting power of the mother–child mediation score. The CITM preteaching score (static) was predicted only by the RCPM scores (first analysis), both tests being static tests. This result verifies what is commonly known in psychometrics: The common variance of two ability tests is higher than the common variance of an ability test (child variable) with an observed behavior (in this case, MLE mother–child interactions). The CITM postteaching score (second analysis) seems to be composed of two components: the previously acquired inferential skills, as manifested in children's CITM preteaching performance, and what has been learned as a result of mediation given by the examiner within the teaching phase. It is plausible to assume that the first component (preteaching score) is attributed to the RCPM score, and the second component (postteaching score) to the mother–child MLE score. In the last analysis, when the gain score (third analysis) was taken as the predicted variable, only the mother–child MLE score emerged as a significant predictive variable. The progression of the predictability pattern across the three regression analyses is quite intriguing as it shows that the more the criterion score is saturated with mediation effects, within the testing DA procedure, the greater is the variance contributed by MLE mother–child interaction. This kind of progression would not be revealed if we used only static tests.

A more sophisticated data analysis was applied in five other studies on different samples of kindergartners (Tzuriel & Ernst, 1990; Tzuriel & Hatzir, 1999) and school age children (Tzuriel & Weiss, 1998; Tzuriel & Weitz, 1998). The first was structural equation modeling (SEM; Joreskog & Sorbom, 1984) and the second hierarchical regression analysis. The DA measures used in these studies were the CATM, CITM, and the Complex Figure (Rey, 1959). In each study one or more tasks were given. Different sets of distal predictive variables were applied (mother's SES, mother's IQ, low birth weight, mother's acceptance or rejection attitudes, amount of time parents stay with their children at home, and children's personality orientation). In two studies (Tzuriel & Ernst, 1990; Tzuriel & Weiss, 1998), an SEM analysis was carried out to test a theoretical model of the effects of distal and proximal factors on cognitive modifiability. The findings of the studies are summarized as follows:

- Children's postteaching scores (dynamic) were predicted by MLE mother–child criteria, whereas the preteaching scores (static) or other static scores were not predicted by any of the mediation scores.
- Mediation for transcendence (i.e., expanding a rule) has emerged as the most powerful predictor of the postteaching scores in all studies. Mediation for meaning predicted preteaching scores in one study (Tzuriel & Ernst, 1990) and mediation for self-regulation predicted postteaching scores in two other studies (Tzuriel & Weiss, 1998; Tzuriel & Weitz, 1998).
- The overall results of the SEM analyses were congruent with the MLE theory according to which proximal factors (i.e., MLE processes) explain individual differences in children's cognitive change, whereas distal factors (e.g., SES-level, child's personality) do not have a direct effect on children's performance on intellective tasks, although they do explain some of the proximal factors.
- Fathers' mediation was as important in predicting children's cognitive performance as was mothers' mediation.
- The lower the children's intellectual level, the higher the benefit from fathers' or mothers' mediation in terms of the cognitive change they show in DA.
- The time parents spend with their children is not sufficient to explain children's cognitive modifiability. It is the quality of interaction (mediation) that explains individual difference in cognitive change.

The findings were explained by referring to both the nature of the specific MLE criteria and the specific cognitive task given in the DA. Parental mediation for transcendence and mediation for self-regulation were found to be important in all studies because performance depends on learning abstract rules, cognitive strategies, and principles such as those taught in the teaching phase and later tested in the postteaching phase. It seems that these two MLE components, acquired during normal mother–child interactions, were assimilated by the children and equipped them with the thinking tools and learning mechanisms that are required later in other tasks and learning settings. When similar mediation for transcendence and self-regulation are provided in other learning situations, these children can retrieve their previous mediation experiences, apply them efficiently with different tasks, and modify their cognitive structures.

The generalizability of these findings should be taken with some caution as they might reflect, at least partially, the compatibility between task characteristics and the context of mother–child mediation. In all studies, the DA tasks used (CATM, Complex Figure, and CITM) require mental strategies and cognitive functions that are similar to the MLE strategies that the mothers used in their interactions within the observed structured situation. One would like to know whether different MLE criteria would evolve as predictive in different situations or as a function of the specific domain tested.

These findings are interpreted as indicating the hypothesized close relationship between adults' mediation and the upper level of their children's zone of proximal development (Vygotsky, 1978), indicated by the postteaching score. These findings also support what both Vygotskian researchers and Feuerstein's DA-approach followers have argued (Tzuriel, 1992a, 2000b, 2001); namely, that the initial performance of a child on intelligence tests often does not reveal the child's potential; that is, his or her ability to modify cognitive structures and thereby to reach higher levels of performance.

DA in Evaluating Cognitive Education Programs

The rationale for using DA in assessing outcomes of cognitive education programs is straightforward: Given that one of the major goals of cognitive education programs is to teach skills of *learning to learn,* it is essential to use DA in which change and improvement criteria can be assessed. We report here research on one cognitive education program: Bright Start.

The Bright Start program. Bright Start (Haywood, Brooks, & Burns, 1986, 1992) was designed for preschool children and children in the early grades of school who experience learning difficulties. The major objectives of Bright Start are as follows: (a) to increase the children's learning effectiveness, (b) to develop efficient cognitive processes and thinking skills, (c) to enhance the development of task-intrinsic motivation, and (d) to prepare children for school learning. Bright Start was designed originally for use with normally developing children who were at high risk of school failure because of socioeconomic disadvantage; however, the target population has been extended to include children who have mild to severe mental retardation, emotional disturbance, autism and pervasive developmental disorders, neurological and sensory impairments, cerebral palsy, and orthopedic handicaps (Haywood, 1995).

Bright Start is not content oriented; rather, it is focused on development of cognitive processes and metacognitive operations that appear to be prerequisite to academic learning in the primary grades. Bright Start is based on a comprehensive theoretical approach synthesized by its authors from several developmental theories. The main theories are Haywood's transactional view of the nature and development of human ability (Haywood, 1995; Haywood, Brooks, et al., 1992; Haywood & Switzky, 1992; Haywood, Tzuriel, et al., 1992) and Feuerstein's theory of structural cognitive modifiability (Feuerstein et al., 1979). Other theoretical sources are Piaget's cognitive–developmental theory and Vygotsky's (1978) socio-cultural theory, especially the concept of the zone of proximal development and the social context for acquisition of cognitive tools.

The effects of Bright Start on children's cognitive modifiability, using DA measures, have been investigated in a series of studies. We present here only the work of Tzuriel, Kaniel, Kanner, and Haywood (1999) as representative of this body of evaluation research because it illustrates the use of DA in program evaluation. In this study kindergartners who had Bright Start in their classrooms ($n = 82$) were compared to children ($n = 52$) who received a basic skills (noncognitive) curriculum, using both static and DA tests. Two DA instruments were administered before and after the intervention: the CATM and the Complex Figure version for young children (Tzuriel & Eiboshitz, 1992). The initial performance on these two tasks was significantly lower for the Bright Start children than for those in the comparison group. Unfortunately, there was no possibility of random assignment of children in each class to experimental and comparison groups without raising resentment from parents. It also would have been confusing to the kindergarten teacher who would have had to implement both programs within one class. The initial scores on the DA tests and the RCPM served as the baseline for comparison of improvement as a function of treatment.

The Bright Start program was applied for 10 months, during which the experimental children received five of the seven small-group units: self-regulation, quantitative relations (number concepts), comparison, classification, and role-taking. The small-group lessons were taught three times a week, each session for a period of 20 min, for a total of 60 min per week, and a total number of 32 hr for the academic year. (Note: This was a much less intensive intervention than is recommended by the program's authors.) The comparison group was given the basic skills program during the academic year and the teachers were visited periodically to observe their skills-based program. At the end of the program, and in a follow-up study after one year, all children were given static and DA tests.

The Bright Start children improved their pre- to postintervention performance on two static measures (CATM preteaching Set A and a test of cognitive development) more than did the comparison group. Findings from the Complex Figure test (DA) were more impressive in view of the fact that the visual–motor aspects of the test were remote from the intervention activities in Bright Start. The Complex Figure was administered as a DA measure before and after the intervention. In order to avoid a ceiling effect at the end of the intervention, an easier version (A) of the Complex Figure test was administered before the intervention and a difficult version (B) was administered after the intervention. Each administration included pre- and postteaching scores. Whereas the experimental group increased its overall performance from pre- ($M = 33.94$) to postintervention ($M = 48.52$), the comparison group showed a decrease from pre- ($M = 42.93$) to postintervention ($M = 39.99$).

Given that mediated learning processes were central in the Bright Start program, it was expected that children would show higher skills of learning to learn than would those in a comparison group. A follow-up study was carried out with both groups in Grade 1 (no further cognitive education after kindergarten), using tests of reading comprehension and math achievement. These tests were administered in addition to DA and static tests. All tests were administered one year after the children had left the program and entered first grade in school.

The results of the follow-up study confirmed the effectiveness of Bright Start in developing learning skills. The Bright Start children scored higher than did the comparison children not only in the preteaching phase of the DA tests but also in the postteaching phase. In spite of the fact that both groups received the same amount of teaching (mediation) within the DA procedure, the Bright Start group continued to show superiority over the comparison group suggesting a greater ability to benefit from mediated instruction. Similarly, scores on the CATM showed that although the comparison group scored somewhat higher than did the experimental group at the end of kindergarten, in the follow-up phase, the experimental group was significantly higher than the comparison group. Moreover, the experimental group showed higher improvement from pre- to postteaching than did the comparison group in the follow-up phase. This result was interpreted as an indication of a snowball effect of the learning to learn treatment: Treatment effects gain power with time without any additional treatment, which is to be expected when the treatment is designed to enhance learning to learn skills.

A second set of analyses was carried out on cognitive modifiability indices that were based on the residual postteaching scores after controlling for the preteaching score (performed separately on the CATM and the Complex Figure scores). The experimental group showed greater improvement in cognitive modifiability scores than the comparison group, from kindergarten to first grade. It should be noted that Bright Start does not include any specifically visual–motor exercises. Rather, the whole program is based on visual presentation of stimuli, discussion of strategies for solving problems, metacognitive processes, verbal dialogues, social interactions, and analyses of situations and problems. In spite of the verbal–logical nature of the program, the most impressive results are those found on the Complex Figure test. Most of the inferences derived from these data sets would not have been possible without the use of DA procedures.

Problems and Conclusions

DA is an innovative approach to assessment of human abilities, especially learning potential. By including teaching (mediation) of basic cognitive concepts and metacognitive operations as a phase of the assessment process, DA avoids the trap of taking knowledge and developed skill as the primary indicator of ability to accomplish future learning. A basic goal of DA is to identify and remove nonintellective barriers to the expression of one's own intelligence, thereby unmasking ability that is already present but frequently not identified by static, normative tests of ability. By reviewing relevant research literature, we have tried to demonstrate that DA is a useful approach in several contexts: psychoeducational assessment of children who are at sociological risk of school failure; assessment of the abilities of culturally different children; and, assessment of abilities of children and others who have special educational needs, including mental retardation, major psychiatric disorders, and traumatic brain injuries.

Although the story we tell here is a positive one, not all is good in the DA world. There are metric problems that have yet to be addressed seriously, much less solved. The question of reliability is a pressing one, especially given that one sets out deliberately to change the very characteristics that are being assessed. At least a partial solution is to insist on very high reliability of the tasks used in DA when they are given in a static mode; that is, without interpolated mediation. Another persistent problem is how to establish the validity of DA. Ideally, one would use both static testing and DA with one group of children and static, normative ability tests with another group. The essential requirement would be that a subgroup of the DA children would have to be given educational experiences that reflected the within-test mediation that helped them to achieve higher performance in DA. The expectation would be that static tests would predict quite well the school achievement of both the static testing group and that subsample of the DA group that did not get cognitive educational follow up. Static tests should predict less well the achievement of the DA-cognitive education group; in fact, the negative predictions made for that group should be defeated to a significant degree.

Other problems are less formal. The professional skill necessary to perform DA effectively is not currently taught in typical graduate psychology programs, so practitioners must be trained in intensive workshops long after they have been indoctrinated in the laws of static, normative testing. Even with excellent training, DA examiners must exercise considerable subjective judgment in determining (a) what cognitive functions are deficient and require mediation, (b) what kinds of mediation to dispense, (c) when further mediation is not needed, and (d) how to interpret the difference between pre-mediation and postmediation performance. Thus, interexaminer agreement is essential. This aspect has been studied to some extent (e.g., Tzuriel & Samuels, 2000) but not yet sufficiently.

One might well ask: Why, if DA is so rich and rewarding, is it not more widely applied (e.g., Elliott, 1993; Tzuriel, 2000b, 2001, 2002)? One apparent reason is that it is not yet taught in graduate school. A second reason is that school psychologists often have client quotas to fill, and since DA is far more time-consuming than is static testing, their supervisors do not permit it. Third, the school personnel who ultimately receive the psychologists' reports typically do not expect DA and do not yet know how to interpret the data or the recommendations, and psychologists offer little help in interpreting the score. Finally, there is a certain inertia inherent in our satisfaction with being able to do what we already know how to do, and to do it exceptionally well. Even so, as we have observed before, "what is not worth doing is not worth doing well!"

References

Benjamin, L., & Lomofsky, L. (2002). Effects of the observation of dynamic and static assessment on teachers' perceptions of the learning potential of less academic learners. *Journal of Cognitive Education and Psychology*, 2(2), 102–123 (online: http://www.iace.coged.org/journal)

Binet, A. (1911). *Les idées modernes sur les enfants [Contemporary ideas on children]*. Paris: Flammarion. (Reedited and republished in 1973, with a preface by Jean Piaget.)

Brown, A. L., & Ferrara, R. A. (1985). Diagnosing zones of proximal development. In J. Wertsch (Ed.), *Culture, communication, and cognition: Vygotskian perspectives* (pp. 272–305). New York: Cambridge University Press.

Budoff, M. (1987). Measures for assessing learning potential. In C. S. Lidz (Ed.), *Dynamic assessment* (pp. 173–195). New York: Guilford.

Burns, S. (1991). Comparison of two types of dynamic assessment with young children. *The International Journal of Dynamic Assessment and Instruction*, 2, 29–42.

Carlson, J. S., & Wiedl, K. H. (1992). The dynamic assessment of intelligence. In H.C. Haywood, & D. Tzuriel, (Eds.), *Interactive assessment* (pp. 167–186). New York: Springer.

Cronbach, L. J. (1970). *Essentials of psychological testing*. New York: Harper & Row.

Delclos, V. R., Vye, N. J., Burns, M. S., Bransford, J. D., & Hasselbring, T. S. (1992). Improving the quality of instruction: Roles for dynamic assessment. In H. C. Haywood & D. Tzuriel (Eds.), *Interactive assessment* (pp. 317–331). New York: Springer.

Elliott, J. (1993). Assisted Assessment: If it is dynamic why is it so rarely employed? *Educational and Child Psychology, 10,* 48–58.

Feuerstein, R., Haywood, H. C., Rand, Y., Hoffman, M. B., & Jensen, M. (1986). *Examiner manual for the Learning Potential Assessment Device.* Jerusalem: Hadassah-WIZO-Canada Research Institute.

Feuerstein, R., Rand, Y., & Hoffman, M. B. (1979). *The dynamic assessment of retarded performers: The learning potential assessment device: Theory, instruments, and techniques.* Baltimore: University Park Press.

Freeman, F. S. (1950). *Theory and practice of psychological testing*. New York: Holt.

Gordon, J. B., & Haywood, H. C. (1969). Input deficit in cultural-familial retardates: Effect of stimulus enrichment. *American Journal of Mental Deficiency, 73,* 604–610.

Guthke, J. (1992). Learning tests: The concept, main research findings, problems, and trends. In J. S. Carlson (Ed.), *Advances in cognition and educational practice, 1A* (pp. 213–233). Greenwich, CT: JAI.

Guthke, J., & Al-Zoubi, A. (1987). Kulturspezifische differenzen in den Colored Progressive Matrices (CPM) und in einer Lenrtestvariante der CPM [Specific cultural differences in the Colored Progressive Matrices (CPM) and in a CPM Lerntest variation]. *Psychologie in Erziehung und Unterricht, 34,* 306–311.

Guthke, J., & Wingenfeld, S. (1992). The learning test concept: Origins, state of the art, and trends. In H. C. Haywood & D. Tzuriel (Eds.), *Interactive assessment* (pp. 64–93). New York: Springer.

Gutkin, T. B., & Reynolds, C. R. (1980). Factorial similarity of the WISC-R for Anglos and Chicanos referred for psychological services. *Journal of School Psychology, 18,* 34–39.

Hamers, J. H. M., Hessels, M. G. P., & van Luit, J. E. H. (1991). *Leertest voor etnische minderheden: Test en handleiding [Learning potential test for ethnic minorities: Test and manual].* Lisse, Netherlands: Swets & Zeitlinger.

Haywood, H. C. (1977a). Alternatives to normative assessment. In P. Mittler (Ed.), *Research to practice in mental retardation: Proceedings of the 4th Congress of the International Association for the Scientific Study of Mental Deficiency, Vol. 2, Education and training* (pp. 11–18). Baltimore: University Park Press.

Haywood, H. C. (1977b). A cognitive approach to the education of retarded children. *Peabody Journal of Education, 54,* 110–116.

Haywood, H. C. (1986). The Test of Verbal Abstracting (TVA). In R. Feuerstein, H. C. Haywood, Y. Rand, M. B. Hoffman, & M. Jensen, *Examiner manual for the Learning Potential Assessment Device.* Jerusalem: Hadassah-WIZO-Canada Research Institute.

Haywood, H. C. (1992). Interactive assessment: A special issue. *Journal of Special Education, 26,* 233–234.

Haywood, H. C. (1995, November). *Cognitive early education: Confluence of psychology and education.* Paper presented at the Second International Congress on Psychology and Education, Madrid.

Haywood, H. C. (1997). Interactive assessment. In R. Taylor (Ed.), *Assessment of individuals with mental retardation* (pp. 103–129). San Diego, CA: Singular.

Haywood, H. C., Brooks, P. & Burns, S. (1986). Stimulating cognitive development at developmental level: A tested non-remedial preschool curriculum for preschoolers and older retarded children. In M. Schwebel & C. A. Maher (Eds.), *Facilitating cognitive development: Principles, practices, and programs* (pp. 127–147). New York: Haworth Press.

Haywood, H. C., Brooks, P. H., & Burns, S. (1992). *Bright Start: Cognitive Curriculum for Young Children.* Watertown, MA: Charles Bridge.

Haywood, H. C., Filler, J. W., Shifman, M. A., & Chatelanat, G. (1975). Behavioral assessment in mental retardation. In P. McReynolds (Ed.), *Advances in psychological assessment* (Vol. 3, pp. 96–136). San Francisco: Jossey-Bass.

Haywood, H. C., & Miller, M. B. (2002, May). *Dynamic assessment of persons with traumatic brain injuries: A pilot study.* Paper given at the European Regional conference of the International Association for Cognitive Education, Rimini, Italy.

Haywood, H. C., & Paour, J.-L. (1992). Alfred Binet (1857–1911): Multifaceted pioneer. *Psychology in Mental Retardation and Developmental Disabilities, 18,* 1–4.

Haywood, H. C., & Switzky, H. N. (1992). Ability and modifiability: What, how, and how much? In J. S. Carlson (Ed.), *Cognition and educational practice: An international perspective* (pp. 25–85). Greenwich, CT: JAI.

Haywood, H. C., & Tzuriel, D. (Eds.). (1992). *Interactive assessment.* New York: Springer-Verlag.

Haywood, H. C., Tzuriel, D., & Vaught, S. (1992). Psycheducational assessment from a transactional perspective. In H. C. Haywood & D. Tzuriel (Eds.), *Interactive assessment* (pp. 38–63). New York: Springer.

Haywood, H. C., & Wingenfeld, S. (1992). Interactive assessment as a research tool. *Journal of Special Education, 26,* 253–268.

Heinrich, J. J. (1991). *Responsiveness of adults with severe head injury to mediated learning.* Unpublished doctoral dissertation, Vanderbilt University.

Hessels, M. G. P. (1997). Low IQ but high learning potential: Why Zeyneb and Moussa do not belong in special education. *Educational and Child Psychology, 14,* 121–136.

Hessels, M. G. P., & Hamers, J. H. M. (1993). A learning potential test for ethnic minorities. In J. H. M. Hamers & A. J. J. M. Ruijssenaars (Eds.), *Learning potential assessment* (pp. 285–312). Amsterdam: Swets & Zeitlinger.

Jensen, A. R. (1980). *Bias in mental testing.* New York: Free Press.

Jensen, A. R. (1985). The nature of Black–White differences on various psychometric tests. *Behavioral and Brain Sciences, 8,* 359–368.

Joreskog, K. G., & Sorbom, D. (1984). *LISREL VI: Analysis of linear structural relationships by the method of maximum likelihood.* Chicago: National Educational Resources.

Kaniel, S., Tzuriel, D., Feuerstein, R., Ben-Shachar, N., & Eitan, T. (1991). Dynamic assessment, learning, and transfer abilities of Jewish Ethiopian immigrants to Israel. In R. Feuerstein, P. S. Klein, & A. Tannenbaum (Eds.), *Mediated learning experience* (pp. 179–209). London: Freund.

Kester, E. S., & Peña, E. D. (2001). Outcomes of dynamic assessment with culturally and linguistically diverse students: A comparison of three teaching methods within a test–teach–test framework. *Journal of Cognitive Education and Psychology, 2,* 42–49. (online: http://www.iacep.coged.org/journal)

Köhler, W. (1917). *Intelligenzprüfungen an Anthropoiden [Intelligence testing of anthropoids].* Berlin: Springer-Verlag.

Lidz, C. S. (1992). Extent of incorporation of dynamic assessment in cognitive assessment courses: A national survey of school psychology trainers. *Journal of Special Education, 26,* 325–331.

Luria, A. R. (1976). *The working brain* (B. Haigh, Trans.). New York: Basic Books.

Miller, M. B. (2002). *Verbal Memory Test to accompany the TVA.* Unpublished report. Patterson, NY: United Cerebral Palsy of Putnam and Southern Duchess Counties.

Missiuna, C., & Samuels, M. (1989). Dynamic assessment of preschool children with special needs: Comparison of mediation and instruction. *Remedial and Special Education, 10,* 53–62.

Osterrieth, P.-A. (1944). Le Test de Copie d'Une Figure Complex: Contribution à l'étude de la perception et de la mémoire [The Complex Figure Test: Contribution to the study of perception and memory]. *Éditions des Archives de Psychologie.* Neuchâtel, France: Delachaux & Niestlé.

Paour, J.-L. (1992). Induction of logic structures in the mentally retarded: An assessment and intervention instrument. In H. C. Haywood & D. Tzuriel (Eds.), *Interactive assessment* (pp. 119–166). New York: Springer.

Paour, J.-L., & Soavi, G. (1992). A case study in the induction of logic structures. In H. C. Haywood & D. Tzuriel (Eds.), *Interactive assessment* (pp. 419–442). New York: Springer.

Raven, J. C. (1956). *Guide to using the Colored Progressive Matrices, Sets A, Ab, and B.* London: H.K. Lewis.

Reitan, R. M., & Wolfson, D. (1985). *The Halstead–Reitan Neuropsychological Test Battery: Theory and clinical interpretation.* Tucson, AZ: Neuropsychology Press.

Resing, W. C. M. (1997). Learning potential assessment: The alternative for measuring intelligence? *Educational and Child Psychology, 14,* 68–82.

Rey, A. (1934). D'un procédé pour évaluer l'éducabilité (quelques applications en psychopathologie) [A procedure for assessing educability (applications to psychopathology).] *Archives de Psychologie, 24,* 297–337.

Rey, A. (1941). L'Examen psychologique dans les cas d'encéphalopathie traumatique [Psychological assessment in cases of traumatic brain injury]. *Archives de Psychologie, 28*(112).

Rey, A. (1959). *Test de copie et de réproduction de mémoire de figures géométriques complexes [Test of copying and memory reproduction of geometric figures].* Paris: Centre de Psychologie Appliquée.

Sclan, S. G. (1986). *Dynamic assessment and thought disorder in paranoid and nonparanoid schizophrenic patients.* Unpublished doctoral dissertation, Vanderbilt University.

Scribner, S. (1984). Studying working intelligence. In B. Rogoff & J. Lave (Eds.). *Everyday cognition: Its development in social context* (pp. 9–40). Cambridge, MA: Harvard University Press.

Sharpe, D., Cole, M., & Lave, J. (1979). Education and cognitive development: The evidence from experimental research. *Monographs of the Society for Research in Child Development, 44*(1–2, Serial No. 178).

Skuy, M., & Shmukler, D. (1987). Effectiveness of the Learning Potential Assessment Device for Indian and "colored" South Africans. *International Journal of Special Education, 2,* 131–149.

Tzuriel, D. (1989). Inferential cognitive modifiability in young socially disadvantaged and advantaged children. *International Journal of Dynamic Assessment and Instruction, 1,* 65–80.

Tzuriel, D. (1992a). The dynamic assessment approach: A reply to Frisbee and Braden. *Journal of Special Education, 26,* 302–324.

Tzuriel, D. (1992b). *The Children's Inferential Thinking Modifiability (CITM) test—instruction manual.* Ramat-Gan, Israel: School of Education, Bar Ilan University.

Tzuriel, D. (1995). *The Children's Seriational Thinking Modifiability (CSTM) Test—instruction manual.* School of Education, Bar Ilan University.

Tzuriel, D. (1997). A novel dynamic assessment approach for young children: Major dimensions and current research. *Educational and Child Psychology, 14,* 83–108.

Tzuriel, D. (1999). Parent-child mediated learning transactions as determinants of cognitive modifiability: Recent research and future directions. *Genetic, Social, and General Psychology Monographs, 125,* 109–156.

Tzuriel, D. (2000a). The Cognitive Modifiability Battery (CMB)—Assessment and intervention: Development of a dynamic assessment instrument. In C. S. Lidz and J. Elliott (Eds.), *Dynamic assessment: Prevailing models and applications* (pp. 375–406). New York: JAI.

Tzuriel, D. (2000b). Dynamic assessment of young children: Educational and intervention perspectives. *Educational Psychology Review, 12,* 385–435.

Tzuriel, D. (2001). *Dynamic assessment of young children*. New York: Kluwer Academic/Plenum.

Tzuriel, D. (2002). Cognitive education: The menace and hope. In W. Resing, W. Ruijssenaars, & D. Aalsvoort (Eds.), *Learning potential assessment and cognitive training: Actual research perspectives in theory building and methodology* (pp. 355–363). New York: JAI/Elsevier.

Tzuriel, D., & Eiboshitz, Y. (1992). A structured program for visual motor integration (SP–VMI) for preschool children. *Learning and Individual Differences, 4,* 104–123.

Tzuriel, D., & Eran, Z. (1990). Inferential cognitive modifiability as a function of mother–child mediated learning experience (MLE) interactions among Kibbutz young children. *International Journal of Cognitive Education and Mediated Learning, 1,* 103–117.

Tzuriel, D., & Ernst, H. (1990). Mediated learning experience and structural cognitive modifiability: Testing of distal and proximal factors by structural equation model. *International Journal of Cognitive Education and Mediated Learning, 1,* 119–135.

Tzuriel, D., & Hatzir, A. (1999, June). *The effects of mediational strategies of fathers and mothers and amount of time they spent with their young children on children's cognitive modifiability.* Paper presented at the 7th Conference of the International Association for Cognitive Education (IACE), Calgary, Canada.

Tzuriel, D., & Haywood, H. C. (1992). The development of interactive-dynamic approaches for assessment of learning potential. In H. C. Haywood & D. Tzuriel (Eds.), *Interactive assessment* (pp. 3–37). New York: Springer-Verlag.

Tzuriel, D., Kaniel, S., Kanner, A., & Haywood, H. C. (1999). The effectiveness of Bright Start program in kindergarten on transfer abilities and academic achievements. *Early Childhood Research Quarterly, 114,* 111–141.

Tzuriel, D., & Kaufman, R. (1999). Mediated learning and cognitive modifiability: Dynamic assessment of young Ethiopian immigrants in Israel. *Journal of Cross-Cultural Psychology, 13,* 539–552.

Tzuriel, D., & Klein, P. S. (1985). Analogical thinking modifiability in disadvantaged, regular, special education, and mentally retarded children. *Journal of Abnormal Child Psychology, 13,* 539–552.

Tzuriel, D., & Samuels. M. T. (2000). Dynamic assessment of learning potential: Inter-rater reliability of deficient cognitive functions, type of mediation, and non-intellective factors. *Journal of Cognitive Education and Psychology, 1,* 41–64. (online: http://www.iacep.coged.org/journal)

Tzuriel, D., & Weiss, S. (1998). Cognitive modifiability as a function of mother–child mediated learning interactions, mother's acceptance-rejection, and child's personality. *Early Childhood and Parenting, 7,* 79–99.

Tzuriel, D., & Weitz, A. (1998). Mother–child mediated learning experience (MLE) strategies and children's cognitive modifiability among very low birth weight (VLBW) and normally born weight (NBW) children. Unpublished manuscript, School of Education, Bar Ilan University.

Utley, C. A., Haywood, H. C., & Masters, J. C. (1992). Policy implications of psychological assessment of minority children. In H. C. Haywood & D. Tzuriel (Eds.). *Interactive assessment* (pp. 445–469). New York: Springer.

Vye, N. J., Burns, M. S., Delclos, V. R., & Bransford, J. D. (1987). Dynamic assessment of intellectually handicapped children. In C. S. Lidz (Ed.), *Dynamic assessment* (pp. 327–359). New York: Guilford.

Vygotsky, L. S. (1978). *Mind in society.* Cambridge, MA: Harvard University Press.

Vygotsky, L. S. (1986). *Thought and language.* Cambridge, MA: MIT Press (Original work published 1934).

Woodcock, R. W., & Johnson, M. B. (1977). *Woodcock–Johnson Psycho-Educational Battery.* Allen, TX: DLM.

PEABODY JOURNAL OF EDUCATION, 77(2), 64–84

Curriculum-Based Measurement: Describing Competence, Enhancing Outcomes, Evaluating Treatment Effects, and Identifying Treatment Nonresponders

Lynn S. Fuchs and Douglas Fuchs
Peabody College
Vanderbilt University

The authors summarize research on curriculum-based measurement (CBM) within four strands. They provide an overview of studies demonstrating the psychometric tenability of CBM. They discuss the body of work showing how teachers can use CBM to inform instructional planning. They examine CBM's potential use in evaluating treatment effects. Finally, they summarize work on CBM for the purpose of identifying children who fail to profit from otherwise effective instruction.

Curriculum-based measurement (CBM) is a set of methods for indexing academic competence and progress. The goal in developing CBM (Deno, 1985) was to establish a measurement system that teachers could use efficiently to (a) obtain accurate, meaningful information with which to index standing and growth; (b) answer questions about the effectiveness of programs in producing academic learning; and (c) plan better instructional programs. To accomplish this goal, a systematic program of research, conceptualized as a 3 × 3 matrix (Deno & Fuchs, 1987), was undertaken. The rows of this matrix specified questions for developing a measurement system (what to measure, how to measure, and how to use the resulting database); the columns provided criteria that answer those

Requests for reprints should be sent to Lynn S. Fuchs and Douglas Fuchs, Peabody College, Box 330, Nashville, TN 37203.

questions (technical adequacy, treatment validity, and feasibility). A 20-year research program, undertaken by independent investigators at multiple sites, has addressed the cells in this matrix, with multiple studies for reading, spelling, mathematics, and written expression.

In each academic area, CBM integrates key concepts from traditional measurement theory and the conventions of classroom-based observational methodology to forge an innovative approach to assessment. As with traditional measurement, every assessment samples a relatively broad range of skills by sampling each dimension of the annual curriculum on each weekly test; consequently, each repeated measurement is an alternate form, of equivalent difficulty, assessing the same constructs. This sampling strategy differs markedly from typical classroom-based assessment methods, in which teachers assess mastery on a single skill, and after mastery is demonstrated, move on to a different, presumably more difficult skill (L. S. Fuchs & Deno, 1991; L. S. Fuchs & Fuchs, 1999). CBM also relies on a traditional psychometric framework by incorporating conventional notions of reliability and validity so the standardized test administration and scoring methods yield accurate and meaningful information.

By sampling broadly with standardized administration and scoring procedures, the CBM score can be viewed as a *performance indicator.* That is, the CBM score produces a broad dispersion of scores across individuals of the same age, with rank orderings that correspond to important external criteria; it represents an individual's global level of competence in the domain. Practitioners can use this performance indicator to identify discrepancies in performance levels between individuals and peer groups, which helps inform decisions about the need for special services or the point at which decertification and reintegration of students with disabilities occur.

At the same time, however, CBM departs from conventional psychometric applications by integrating the concepts of standardized measurement and traditional reliability and validity with key features from classroom-based observational methodology: repeated performance sampling, fixed time recording, graphic displays of time-series data, and qualitative descriptions of student performance. Reliance on these classroom-based observational methods permits slope estimates for different time periods and alternative interventions for the same individual; this creates the necessary database for describing growth and testing the effects of different treatments for a given student. Also, when combined with prescriptive decision rules, these time-series analytic methods result in better instruction and learning. Teachers raise goals more often and develop higher expectations (L. S. Fuchs, Fuchs, & Hamlett, 1989a), adapt their instruction more frequently (L. S. Fuchs, Fuchs, & Hamlett, 1989b), they effect better student learning (L. S. Fuchs, Fuchs, Hamlett, & Stecker, 1991).

In addition, because each assessment simultaneously samples the multiple skills embedded in the annual curriculum, CBM can yield qualitative descriptions of student performance to supplement graphed, quantitative analyses of CBM total scores. These diagnostic profiles demonstrate reliability and validity (see, e.g., L. S. Fuchs, Fuchs, Hamlett, & Allinder, 1989; L. S. Fuchs, Fuchs, Hamlett, Thompson, et al., 1994), offer the advantage of being rooted in the local curriculum, provide a framework for improving student programs, and result in teachers planning more varied, specific, and responsive instruction to meet individual student needs (L. S. Fuchs, Fuchs, Hamlett, & Allinder, 1991a).

CBM bridges traditional psychometric and classroom-based observational assessment paradigms to forge an innovative approach to measurement. Through this bridging of frameworks, CBM simultaneously yields information about standing as well as change and about global competence as well as skill-by-skill mastery. CBM can, therefore, be used to answer questions about interindividual differences (e.g., How different is Henry's academic level and growth from that of other students in the class, school, or district?); intra-individual improvement (e.g., How successful is an adapted regular classroom in producing better academic growth for Henry?); and how to strengthen individual student programs (e.g., On which skills in the annual curriculum does Henry require instruction?).

In this article, we summarize research on CBM within four strands: (a) We provide an overview of studies demonstrating the psychometric tenability of CBM. (b) We discuss the body of work demonstrating how teachers can use CBM to inform instructional planning and effect superior learning. (c) We examine CBM's potential use in evaluating treatment effects. (d) We summarize work on CBM for the purpose of identifying children who fail to profit from otherwise effective instruction; that is, the group of students referred to alternately as treatment *resisters* or *nonresponders*.

Psychometric Tenability of CBM

We illustrate the psychometric strengths of CBM by briefly summarizing information in the area of reading. In mathematics, spelling, and written expression, similar data exist; however, the vast majority of independent replications do occur in reading. We organize our discussion in terms of technical features necessary for describing student competence at one time as opposed to the features needed to model student growth over time.

Describing Student Competence at a Specific Time

To provide the basis for sound decision making about a student's performance level, an assessment score (or an average across several scores) must provide an accurate and meaningful estimate of competence; therefore, traditional psychometric methods for investigating technical adequacy apply. To achieve these traditional psychometric criteria, assessment methods typically sample behavior broadly, rely on standardized administration and scoring procedures, and accordingly are viewed as performance indicators. This is the case for CBM, which illustrates how a classroom-based assessment method can achieve traditional psychometric standards.

In reading, two CBM measures are the number of words read aloud from text in 1 min and the number of correct replacements restored to text from which every seventh word has been deleted in 2.5 min. Each measure demonstrates strong criterion validity with respect to widely used, commercial reading tests (L. S. Fuchs & Fuchs, 1992; Marston, 1989), to informal reading measures involving question answering, close completion, recall of passages (L. S. Fuchs & Fuchs, 1992; L. S. Fuchs, Fuchs, & Maxwell, 1988), and to teachers' judgments of reading competence (L. S. Fuchs & Fuchs, 1992; L. S. Fuchs, Fuchs, & Deno, 1982). In addition, evidence suggests adequate (a) predictive validity (e.g., D. Fuchs, Fuchs, Thompson, et al., 2001), and construct validity (e.g., Shinn, Good, Knutson, Tilly, & Collins, 1992), (b) discriminative validity with respect to special education status (Deno, Mirkin, & Chiang, 1982; Shinn, Tindal, Spira, & Marston, 1987) and grade (Deno, 1985; L. S. Fuchs & Deno, 1992; L. S. Fuchs, Fuchs, Hamlett, Walz, & Germann, 1993), (c) stability (L. S. Fuchs, Deno, & Marston, 1983; L. S. Fuchs & Fuchs, 1992), and (d) interscorer agreement (L. S. Fuchs, Fuchs, Hamlett, & Ferguson, 1992; Marston & Deno, 1981).

In the most recent study of CBM's psychometric features, Hosp and Fuchs (2001) had 74 first graders, 81 second graders, 79 third graders, and 75 fourth graders read two CBM grade-appropriate passages; they had the students complete the Woodcock Reading Mastery Tests and the word identification, word attack, and passage comprehension subtests; and they re-administered the CBM passages 2–3 weeks later to a subsample of the participants (i.e., 29, 30, 30, and 30 at the four grades, respectively). At these respective grades, criterion validity between CBM and word identification was .89, .88, .89, and .79; between CBM and word attack, .70, .82, .82, and .74; and between CBM and passage comprehension, .76, .83, .83, and .83. Test–retest reliability was .96, .97, .93, and .93. In another study (Fuchs & Hamlett, 1997), predictive validity with respect to a commercial group-administered achievement test, the TerraNova, was .86 over 12 weeks (January–April) as documented among 324 first-grade students; .79 over 30 weeks (October–May) as documented among 87 second-grade students; and .72 over 30 weeks (October–May) as documented among 95 third-grade students.

Modeling Academic Growth

Performance indicators, which are commonly associated with formal testing, are also important to the classroom-based assessment methods, such as CBM, for modeling growth. This is the case for two reasons: (a) Performance indicators provide a broad range of scores required for manifesting change over time and (b) the traditional standards of psychometric adequacy on which performance indicators are based provide necessary evidence for presuming that differences between an individual's data points represent meaningful change.

Unfortunately, however, these traditional psychometric criteria are insufficient evidence that a measure can adequately depict growth. The modeling of longitudinal data to describe growth has been discussed for some time in the biological and statistical literatures and has been applied more recently in psychology (e.g., Willett, Ayoub, & Robinson, 1991) and education. As discussed by Francis, Shaywitz, Stuebing, Shaywitz, and Fletcher (1994), instruments for longitudinally modeling individual change must demonstrate certain technical features, which CBM demonstrates.

First, the instrument must provide equal scaling of individuals throughout the range of behavior measured over time (i.e., produce data with interval scale properties, free from ceiling or floor effects). With CBM, a common test framework is administered to children within a fixed age range, making it possible to judge performance over an academic year on the same raw score metric. When performance is measured on the appropriate instructional level of the curriculum, floor and ceiling effects do not occur. Second, the construct and the difficulty level measured over time must remain constant. CBM taps constructs that are qualitatively constant over an academic year, for which the difficulty level remains the same. The third technical requirement for the modeling of growth is that a sufficient number of alternate forms be available to obtain accurate estimates of change parameters. With CBM, alternate passages of constant difficulty are available (9–30 passages per grade, depending on source), and research (L. S. Fuchs, 1993) suggests that approximately 7 data points are adequate for fitting data to a model.

Current techniques for measuring change reconceptualize growth as a continuous, rather than an incremental, process. The goal is to describe trajectories, or continuous time-dependent curves, which reflect the change process. An initial step in such a process is to formulate a change model at the individual level. Examination of individual and group time-series CBM data provides the basis for an empirical approximation of the shape of CBM growth curves (Francis et al., 1994). L. S. Fuchs, et al. (1993), for example, examined students' academic growth rates when CBM was conducted for one school year in students' grade-appropriate curriculum level. For many students on each CBM measure, a linear relationship adequately modeled student progress within one academic year. When significant quadratic terms occurred (for 0%–21% of students), growth was almost consistently described by a negatively accelerating pattern, in which student performance continues to improve over the course of a year, but the amount of that progress gradually decreases. As suggested in cross-sectional data, this negatively accelerating pattern may also characterize growth across academic years. These findings, in combination with corroborating evidence (Good, Deno, & Fuchs, 1995; Good & Shinn, 1990), support a conceptualization of annual CBM growth characterized by a linear relationship, where slope is a primary parameter describing change. Consequently, CBM appears to be a tenable measurement tool for modeling academic growth.

Using CBM to Enhance Instructional Planning and Student Learning

A well-established, long-standing research program documents how CBM can help teachers plan better instruction and effect superior achievement. Several investigators have examined the effects of alternative data-utilization strategies, as well as CBM's overall contribution to instructional planning and student learning, not only in regular educationbut in special education as well.

Effects of Alternative Data-Utilization Strategies

CBM has been shown to enhance teacher planning and student learning by helping teachers set ambitious student goals, by assisting teachers in determining when instructional adaptations are necessary to prompt better student growth, and by providing ideas for potentially effective teaching adjustments.

Setting ambitious goals. Studies illustrate how teachers may use CBM to help them establish ambitious goals, which result in accelerated student learning. Fuchs, Fuchs, and Hamlett (1989a), for example, explored the contribution of goal-raising guidelines within CBM decision-making rules. Teachers were assigned randomly to and participated in one of three treatments for 15 weeks in mathematics: no CBM, CBM without a goal-raising rule, and CBM with a goal-raising rule. The goal-raising rule required teachers to increase goals whenever the student's actual rate of growth, represented by an ordinary least squares regression through at least 7 CBM scores, was greater than the growth rate anticipated by the teacher. Teachers in the CBM goal-raising condition raised goals more frequently (for 15 of 30 students) than did teachers in the nongoal-raising conditions (for 1 of 30 students); moreover, concurrent with teachers' goal raising was differential student achievement on pre- and poststandardized achievement tests: The effect size comparing the pre- and post-change of the two CBM conditions (i.e., with and without the goal-raising rule) was .52 standard deviations. Using CBM to monitor the appropriateness of instructional goals and adjust goals upward whenever possible represents one means by which teachers can use CBM to enhance their instructional planning.

Identifying when to revise the instructional program. A second way in which CBM can be used to enhance instructional decision making is to assess the adequacy of student progress and determine whether, and if so when, instructional adaptation is necessary. When the actual growth rate (ordinary least squares regression line through at least 7 CBM scores) is less than the expected growth rate (slope of the goal line), the teacher modifies the instructional program to promote stronger learning. L. S. Fuchs, et al. (1989b) estimated the contribution of this CBM decision-making strategy with 29 special educators who implemented CBM for 15 school weeks with 53 students with mild to moderate disabilities. Teachers in a CBM-measurement only group measured students' reading growth as required but did not use the assessment information to structure students' reading programs. Teachers in the CBM-change the program decision-rule group measured student performance and used the assessment information to determine when to introduce programmatic adaptations to enhance growth rates. Results indicated that although teachers in both groups measured student performance, important differences were associated with the use of the change the program decision rule. As indicated on the Stanford Achievement Test–reading comprehension subtest, students in the change the program decision-rule group achieved better than did a no-CBM control group (effect size = .72), whereas the measurement only CBM group did not (effect size = .36). The slopes of the two CBM treatment groups were significantly different, favoring the achievement of the change the program group (effect size = .86). As suggested by these findings and the results of other researchers (e.g., Stecker & Fuchs, 1999; Wesson, Skiba, Sevcik, King, & Deno, 1984), collecting CBM data, in and of itself, exerts only a small effect on student learning. To enhance student outcomes in important ways, teachers need to use the CBM data instrumentally to build effective programs for difficult-to-teach students.

Using CBM diagnostic information to plan instruction. To help teachers determine when adjustments are required in students' programs, thus to identify when goal increases are warranted, the CBM total scores are used. In addition, by inspecting the graph of performance indicators over time, teachers may formulate ideas for potentially effective instructional adaptations. For example, a flat or decelerating slope might generate hypotheses about lack of maintenance of previously learned material or about motivational problems; nevertheless, to obtain rich descriptions of student performance, alternative ways of summarizing and describing student performance are necessary. Because CBM assesses performance on the year's curriculum at each testing, rich descriptions of strengths and weaknesses in the curriculum can be generated.

During the 1987–1988 academic year, we investigated the contribution of these CBM diagnostic profiles in math (L. S. Fuchs, et al., 1991), reading (L. S. Fuchs, Fuchs, & Hamlett, 1989c), and spelling (L. S. Fuchs, Fuchs, Hamlett, & Allinder, 1991a). In each investigation, teachers were assigned randomly to one of three conditions: no CBM, CBM with goal-raising and change-the-program decision rules, and CBM with goal-raising and change-the-program decision rules along with CBM diagnostic profiles. In all three studies, teachers in the diagnostic profile treatment group generated instructional plans that were more varied and more responsive to individuals' learning needs. Moreover, they effected better student learning as measured on change between pre- and posttest performance on global measures of achievement. Effect sizes associated with the CBM diagnostic profile groups ranged from .65 to 1.23. This series of studies demonstrated how structured, well-organized CBM information about students' strengths and difficulties in the curriculum helps teachers build better programs and effect greater learning.

More recently, we explored additional methods for deriving additional diagnostic information from the CBM reading aloud score. The first step in this research program was to identify CBM cut-points, by grade level, at which students required decoding versus fluency versus comprehension intervention. To accomplish this, Hosp and Fuchs (2001) had 74 first graders, 81 second graders, 79 third graders, and 75 fourth graders read two CBM grade-appropriate passages; they had students complete the Woodcock Reading Mastery Tests word identification, word attack, and passage comprehension subtests; and they had students complete the Decoding Skills Battery (Fuchs, Hosp, Fuchs, & Hamlett, 2001b), which assesses student mastery of 10 decoding skills. Using discriminant function analyses on CBM, the Decoding Skills Battery, and Woodcock performance, we established the cut-points. Teachers then used CBM in conjunction with the Decoding Skills Battery to plan instruction in the following way. Every 3 weeks, students were categorized, using their most recent CBM score, into decoding-, fluency-, or comprehension-building activities. For students classified as requiring decoding work, the Decoding Skills Battery was administered (1–5 min using basals and ceilings) to categorize students further into the decoding skills on which instruction should occur. Fuchs, Hosp, Fuchs, and Hamlett (2001a) are investigating the effects of this CBM diagnostic feedback among 28 second-grade teachers who were assigned randomly to four groups: control, instructional consultation, instructional consultation with CBM, and instructional consultation with CBM plus diagnostic feedback. Effects are being assessed on instructional planning and student learning.

CBM's Overall Contribution to Teacher Planning and Student Achievement in Regular Classrooms

As described by Marston and Magnusson (1988), the Minneapolis Public Schools incorporated CBM prereferral assessment within its eligibility assessment process. Over a period of 6 weeks, interventions were implemented and ongoing CBM data were collected to assess the extent to which students' academic needs could be addressed in the regular classroom when instructional adaptations had been introduced. Only pupils whose performance did not improve as a function of these adaptations were identified for special education services. Marston and Magnusson (1988) reported that among students initially referred, 25–45% were deemed eligible for special education after CBM prereferral assessment. This figure is dramatically lower than the estimate reported by Algozzine, Christenson, and Ysseldyke (1982), in which 90% of referred students were subsequently identified for special education using conventional assessment procedures.

During the 1992–1993 school year, L. S. Fuchs, Fuchs, Hamlett, Phillips, and Karns (1995) further studied the viability of CBM prereferral assessment. We randomly assigned general educators to two treatments. In both treatments, teachers implemented CBM in mathematics with all students in their classes beginning in September. In addition, to facilitate the link between CBM and instruction, teachers in both conditions incorporated a demonstrably effective structured form of peer-assisted learning (e.g., D. Fuchs, Fuchs, Mathes, & Simmons, 1997; L. S. Fuchs, Fuchs, Hamlett, Phillips, et al., 1997).

This combination of CBM and peer-assisted learning strategies therefore represented the baseline treatment in this study, over which individual instructional adaptations were layered. Beginning in November, the bimonthly CBM class reports identified up to two target students per class whose CBM progress was inadequate (i.e., low level combined with low slope, relative to classmates). For these students, teachers (a) formulated an adaptation before the next 2-week report, (b) implemented that adaptation at least four times in the upcoming 2 weeks, and (c) modified previous adaptations to enhance progress when CBM identified the same student over multiple reports.

Results demonstrated that when general educators are specifically prompted with CBM and supported to engage in instructional adaptation, they do so with respectable fidelity. Across three to six 2-week adaptation cycles, teachers ignored requests for adaptations only infrequently; they often implemented multiple strategies concurrently to address the problems of target students; and some teachers modified student programs repeatedly in a variety of ways in an attempt to boost progress. Moreover, teacher reliance on individual adaptations appeared to prompt changes in their thinking about differentiating instructional plans. Compared to teachers in the baseline treatment, those in the adaptations treatment reported (a) more modifications in their goals and strategies for poorly progressing students, (b) a greater variety of skills taught, (c) selective reteaching of lessons more frequently, and (d) more frequent deviation from the teacher's manual for selected students.

Findings were not uniformly positive, however. Despite many focused attempts to enhance learning, some children proved unresponsive to regular classroom adaptations. Two brief cases illustrate this differential responsiveness. Over a 12-week period, a fourth-grade teacher implemented a rich set of adaptations, relying on basic facts drills, motivational workcharts and contracts, and manipulatives. The target student, who exhibited a CBM slope of .21 digits per week when identified for adaptation, responded well to these modifications to the regular classroom and completed the school year with a slope of .63 digits per week—the average slope for the class. This success contrasts with the experience of a third-grade teacher who also implemented a large number of adaptations including drilling basic facts, sliding back to second-grade material, implementing a motivational workchart, and using money to work on conceptual underpinnings. Despite this teacher's similar level of effort to modify regular classroom instruction, her target student demonstrated little improvement in growth rate: He ended the year with a relatively low slope of .28 digits per week, which was similar to his slope at the time he was identified for adaptation and which was considerably lower than his classmates' average slope of .98 digits per week.

Three of our 10 teachers effected substantial improvement for target students. This suggests that, with the assistance of rich assessment information and consultative support to formulate feasible adaptations, regular classroom teachers may be able to address the problems of some portion (in this case, 30%) of students who initially demonstrate significant learning discrepancies from classroom peers. Nevertheless, this database simultaneously indicates that some students will remain unresponsive to an adapted general education environment. This unresponsiveness creates the need for additional resources—specifically, the individualized instruction, the small-size instructional groups, and the more highly trained teachers available through special education—to address the learning problems of a small portion of learners.

Teacher Planning and Student Achievement in Special Education

Evidence supporting CBM's utility in helping special educators plan more effective programs is strong. Corroborating evidence (e.g., L. S. Fuchs, Deno, & Mirkin, 1984; L. S. Fuchs, et al., 1991a; L. S. Fuchs, et al., 1992; Jones & Krouse, 1988; Stecker & Fuchs, 1999; Wesson, Skiba, et al., 1984; Wesson, 1991) shows dramatic effects on student outcomes in reading, spelling, and math when special educators rely on CBM to inform instructional planning. To illustrate this database, we briefly describe one study in reading.

L. S. Fuchs et al. (1984) conducted a study in the New York City Public Schools. Teachers participated for 18 weeks in a contrast group or a CBM treatment group, where teachers conducted reading CBM at least twice weekly, scored and graphed those performances, and used prescriptive CBM decision rules for planning the students' reading programs. Children whose teachers employed CBM to develop reading programs achieved better than students whose teachers used conventional monitoring methods on the Passage Reading Test and on the decoding and comprehension subtests of the Stanford Diagnostic Reading Test. Respective effect sizes were 1.18, .94, and .99. This suggests that, despite CBM's focus on text reading fluency, teachers planned better reading programs comprehensively to include foci on fluency, decoding, and comprehension.

Evaluating Treatment Effectiveness

To function adequately as a tool for evaluating treatment effectiveness, CBM must be able to answer questions such as the following: Is the regular classroom environment producing adequate growth? Do adaptations introduced in the regular classroom setting result in an improved growth rate? Does the provision of specialized services enhance student learning? To answer these treatment effectiveness questions, the assessment must demonstrate sensitivity to student growth and to relative treatment effects, and it must permit comparisons of the effectiveness of alternative service delivery options. CBM demonstrates these features.

Sensitivity to Academic Change

In an early study devoted to the issue of sensitivity to academic change, Marston, Fuchs, and Deno (1986) tested students on traditional, commercial achievement tests and on curriculum-based reading and written language measures early in October and 10 weeks later in December. CBM registered more student growth than did the traditional tests, suggesting greater sensitivity to student growth. In an operational replication, published as a second study in the same article, Marston et al. corroborated findings with pre- and posttestings 16 weeks apart on traditional, commercial reading achievement.

Other research has directly compared the sensitivity of CBM pre- and postperformance levels to that of CBM slopes. For example, while investigating the effects of a 3-week winter break on students' math performance, Allinder and Fuchs (1994) contrasted (a) comparison of CBM performance levels before and after the break with (b) comparison of pre- and postbreak slopes of progress. Results differed by type of analysis: Effects of the break were not demonstrated when performance level was assessed; examination of slopes, however, showed that students with positive prebreak trends were affected adversely by the school break, whereas students with negative prebreak trends were not.

Studies have also demonstrated that slopes based on ongoing CBM data reflect treatment effects more sensitively than traditional measures administered on a pre- and postbasis. L. S. Fuchs, et al. (1989b) showed that on the Stanford Achievement Test–reading comprehension subtest, administered to detect incremental change between two points in time, change scores of the treatment groups were not significantly different, and the effect size was a relatively low .36. By contrast, on CBM slope data, differences between groups achieved statistical significance and were associated with a larger effect size of .86 standard deviations. This pattern showing substantially larger effect sizes for CBM slope data has been corroborated in other treatment effectiveness research (e.g., L. S. Fuchs, et al., 1991; L. S. Fuchs, Fuchs, Hamlett, Phillips, & Bentz, 1994). Evidence therefore suggests that CBM slopes may be sensitive to student growth and to the relative effects of alternative treatments.

Comparing Student Progress under
Alternative Service Delivery Options

Given a sensitive measurement system, however, questions remain about how that system functions when comparing student progress under alternative service delivery options. Two CBM studies illustrate this type of decision making. Marston (1987–1988) compared the relative effectiveness of regular and special education by analyzing slope on weekly CBM reading scores. An initial pool of 272 fourth, fifth, and sixth graders were selected for the yearlong study on the basis of performance at or below the 15th percentile on the Minneapolis Benchmark Test. The CBM reading performance of these 272 children was measured weekly. The 11 students who (a) spent at least 10 weeks in regular education, (b) were referred to and placed in special education, and (c) spent at least 10 weeks in special education were the focus of the analysis.

To determine the relative treatment effects of the two service delivery arrangements, a repeated measures analysis of variance was applied to the CBM slope data. Slopes were significantly greater in special education than in regular education, with the average slopes increasing from .60 to 1.15 words across the two service delivery settings. For 10 of 11 students, slopes were larger in special education; in 7 of the 10 cases, the difference was dramatic.

In a similar way, D. Fuchs, Fuchs, and Fernstrom (1993) used slope to examine the relative effectiveness of special and regular education for individual students as they moved in the opposite direction: as they reintegrated into general education classrooms. Twenty-one special education students had been randomly assigned to a condition designed to facilitate successful reintegration to regular classroom math instruction through a deliberate and systematic process involving transenvironmental programming and CBM. Special educators used CBM to inform and strengthen their planning in the area of mathematics; at the same time, they monitored the target students' CBM growth and that of three low-performing (but legitimate academic) members of the general education setting. When the target students' performance level approached that of the low-performing peers, reintegration occurred, and the onus for instruction was transferred to the regular classroom teacher. After reintegration, CBM data continued to be collected for the target student and for the low-performing peers in the regular classroom.

Within special education, the experimental students' slopes were significantly greater than that of the low-performing peers. However, after reintegration, the slopes of the target students plunged and were significantly lower than that of the comparison students. On average, 63% of the reintegrated students' CBM data points in regular education fell below trend lines that had been projected on the basis of their growth rates within special education. This compared to only 44% for the comparison peers, and represented a statistically significant difference. As with the Marston (1987–1988) study, this database clearly revealed the effectiveness of the special, over the general, education setting for many (although not all) students. Both studies demonstrate CBM's capacity to document the effects of service delivery options.

Using CBM to Identify Nonresponders

The traditional assessment framework for identifying students with learning disabilities relies on discrepancies between intelligence and achievement tests to operationalize unexpected underachievement. This traditional framework has been scrutinized and attacked due to measurement and conceptual difficulties. An alternative framework for identifying students with learning disabilities that has received increasing interest (see, e.g., Fuchs & Fuchs, 1998), is one in which learning disability is conceptualized as nonresponsiveness to otherwise effective instruction. It requires that special education be considered only when a child's performance reveals a dual discrepancy: The student not only performs below the level demonstrated by classroom peers but also demonstrates a learning rate substantially below that of classmates.

To illustrate the rationale for this focus on dual discrepancies, we have relied on the following example from pediatric medicine. The endocrinologist monitoring a child's physical growth is interested not only in height but also growth velocity over time (Rosenfeld, 1982). Given a child whose current height places him or her below the third percentile, the endocrinologist considers the possibility of underlying pathology and the need to intervene only if, in response to an adequately nurturing environment, the individual's growth trajectory is flatter than that of appropriate comparison groups. Based on long-term, large-scale normative information (Tanner & Davies, 1985), this criterion typically is operationalized at age 7 as an annual growth rate of less than 4 cm. Consequently, the physician judges the 7-year-old who manifests a large discrepancy in height status, but who is nonetheless growing at least 4 cm annually in response to a nurturing environment, to be deriving available benefits from that environment and to be an inappropriate candidate for special intervention.

The endocrinologist's decision-making framework reflects three assumptions. The first assumption is that genetic variations underlie normal development, producing a range of heights across the population. The second assumption is that in response to a nurturing environment, a short but growing child does not present a pathological profile indicative of a need for special treatment to produce growth. Instead, this profile suggests an individual who may legitimately represent the lower end of the normal distribution on height—an individual whose development is commensurate with his or her capacity to grow. The third assumption is that under these circumstances, special intervention is unlikely to increase adult height sufficiently to warrant the risks associated with that intervention. Of course, when questions about the quality of the environment arise, the response is to remove those uncertainties by enhancing nurturance, even with hospitalization (Wolraich, 1996), so growth can be tested under adequate environmental conditions.

Applied to education, this decision-making framework translates into three related propositions. First, because student capacity varies, educational outcomes will differ across the population of learners, and a low-performing child, who is nonetheless learning, may ultimately perform not as well as his or her peers. For example, we do not expect all children to achieve the same degree of reading competence: Some will become scholars of great literature; others will achieve the minimal levels of competence to permit satisfactory employment and successful parenting.

Second, if a low-performing child is learning at a rate similar to the growth rates of other children in the same classroom environment, he or she is demonstrating the capacity to profit from that educational environment. Additional intervention, therefore, is unwarranted, even though a discrepancy in performance level may exist. That is, given the benefits being derived from the classroom instructional environment, the student probably does not require a unique form of instruction and probably is achieving commensurate with his or her capacity to learn. Moreover, the risks and costs associated with entering the special education system are deemed inappropriate and unnecessary because it is unlikely, in light of the growth already occurring, that a different long-term educational outcome could be achieved as a function of that intervention. Of course, the converse is also assumed. When a low-performing child is not manifesting growth in a situation where others are thriving, consideration of special intervention is warranted. Alternative instructional methods must be tested to address the apparent mismatch between the student's learning requirements and those represented in the conventional instructional program.

The third assumption is that when the vast majority of students in a classroom are achieving inadequate growth rates (in comparison to local or national norms), one must question the adequacy of that educational environment before formulating decisions about individual student responsiveness. In that case, classroom intervention aimed at enhancing the overall quality of the instructional program must occur. Growth under more nurturing environmental conditions must be indexed before any child's need for special intervention can be assessed.

Dual discrepancy as an index of *failure to thrive* has considerable intuitive and empirical appeal. This index deals directly with the problem at hand (e.g., poor reading, poor math skills), reflects a dynamic rather than a static approach to learning and assessment, and is data based. CBM is a promising tool for indexing treatment responsiveness due to its capacity to model student growth, to evaluate treatment effects, and to simultaneously inform instructional programming; however, such an identification model is more labor intensive than a traditional framework. It requires (a) assessment of every child in every classroom every week, (b) evaluation of progress on a regular basis, (c) formulating interventions within general education classrooms for children identified as dually discrepant, (d) implementing the interventions with fidelity, and (e) evaluating the effects of the intervention. The question becomes a treatment validity model worth these additional requirements. One way of addressing this question is through empirical comparison with other identification procedures. Speece and her colleagues (Speece & Case, 2001; Speece, Molloy, & Case, 2000) compared the dual discrepancy method to IQ-reading achievement discrepancy and low reading achievement definitions of reading disability in an epidemiological sample of first- and second-grade children to assess the validity of the dual discrepancy approach. The determination of dual discrepancy status was based on CBM collected across 6 months of a school year. The population ($n = 694$) was screened on CBM letter sound fluency (first grade) and reading aloud (second grade) to identify at-risk

(n = 144) and comparison (n = 129) samples. The at-risk children comprised the lowest 25% of children in each class. To form the comparison sample, five children representing a range of skill above the 30th percentile on the screening measures were selected from each class. The at-risk and comparison samples were followed throughout the school year and were administered a minimum of 10 CBM text reading probes to determine dual discrepancy status (CBM–DD). Other measures of intelligence and reading achievement were used to form the IQ-reading achievement discrepancy (IQ–DS) and low reading achievement (LA) groups. Validation measures included phonological processing variables, teachers' ratings of academic competence, problem behaviors, and social skills, age, gender, and race.

The poor reader groups were formed hierarchically. All children who exhibited a dual discrepancy were assigned to the CBM–DD group. Then the remaining children who met the classification criteria were assigned to the IQ–DS group for the first set of comparisons and then to the LA group for the second, and parallel, set of comparisons. Using these procedures, 47 children were identified as CBM–DD, 17 as IQ–DS, and 28 as LA. The prevalence of CBM–DD was 8.1% compared to 5.9% for IQ–DS (based on all children who met the classification criteria regardless of whether they qualified for either of the other groups). By definition, the LA group would reflect approximately 25% of the population because a standard score below 90 on a norm-referenced measure was used as the criterion. Thus, it appeared that the CBM–DD procedures are likely to identify a reasonable number of children as learning disabled assuming that follow-up prevention activities are implemented to reduce false positive intervention.

Importantly, the CBM–DD group exhibited significantly lower reading scores compared to the at-risk and comparison sample children not classified as poor readers. Also, the CBM–DD group, compared to IQ–DS, was more impaired on every measure with the exception of reading and word reading efficiency. There were fewer and more modest differences between CBM–DD and LA. Notably, the CBM–DD group had poorer phonological awareness skills at second grade and were rated lower on academic competence, problem behaviors, and social skills. Interestingly, the four cross-sectional comparisons that used grade (including IQ–DS) suggested that CBM–DD children become more impaired over time. It was also interesting that the CBM–DD group was younger than either of the other poor reader groups, suggesting that dual discrepancy may support early identification and intervention. In addition, the CBM–DD and LA groups each had racial distributions that reflected the proportions of majority and minority children in the schools, whereas the IQ–DS group had a disproportionately high number of majority children.

Consequently, these group comparisons support the construct validity: The CBM–DD group demonstrated more problems in skills that underlie beginning reading, and teachers viewed CBM–DD children as less academically competent and as exhibiting more social and classroom problem behaviors. Further, the dual discrepancy method demonstrated social consequential validity in that decisions to identify children in this manner reflected racial equity. Also, identified children were younger, a consequence valued by educators, and considerably fewer children were identified compared to a low achievement definition. The CBM–DD classification was the only method that reflected favorably on racial equity as well as early identification. Therefore, although additional work clearly is warranted, a treatment validity framework for identifying learning disabilities, using CBM as a measurement tool, represents a promising alternative.

Conclusion

CBM development began in 1972, with a small number of doctoral students working under the direction of Stanley L. Deno at the University of Minnesota, to develop an efficient assessment teachers could use to describe academic competence and growth and to plan more effective instruction. As illustrated by the research we summarized in this article, over the past 2 decades, the number of independent researchers studying CBM has grown as have the applications investigated. At present, CBM appears useful for describing competence, enhancing outcomes, evaluating treatment effects, and identifying treatment nonresponders. Additional research, exploring other uses and providing additional replication, is required, but CBM's potential has been persuasively demonstrated.

References

Algozzine, B., Christenson, S., & Ysseldyke, J. E. (1982). Probabilities associated with the referral to placement process. *Teacher Education and Special Education, 5*(3), 19–23.

Allinder, R. M., & Fuchs, L. S. (1994). Alternative ways of analyzing effects of a short school break on students with and without disabilities. *School Psychology Quarterly, 9,* 145–160.

Deno, S. L. (1985). Curriculum-based measurement: The emerging alternative. *Exceptional Children, 52,* 219–232.

Deno, S. L., & Fuchs, L. S. (1987). Developing curriculum-based measurement systems for data-based special education problem solving. *Focus on Exceptional Children, 19*(8), 1–16.

Deno, S. L., Mirkin, P., & Chiang, B. (1982). Identifying valid measures of reading. *Exceptional Children, 49,* 36–45.

Francis, D. J., Shaywitz, S. E., Stuebing, K. K., Shaywitz, B. A., & Fletcher, J. M. (1994). The measurement of change: Assessing behavior over time and within a developmental context. In Lyon, G. R. (Ed.), *Frames of reference for the assessment of learning disabilities: New views on measurement issues* (pp. 29–58). Baltimore: Brookes.

Fuchs, D., Fuchs, L. S., & Fernstrom, P. J. (1993). A conservative approach to special education reform: Mainstreaming through transenvironmental programming and curriculum-based measurement. *American Educational Research Journal, 30,* 149–178.

Fuchs, D., Fuchs, L. S., Mathes, P., & Simmons, D. (1997). Peer-assisted learning strategies: Making classrooms more responsible to student diversity. *American Educational Research Journal, 34,* 174–206.

Fuchs, D., Fuchs, L. S., Thompson, A., Al-Otaiba, S., Yen, L., Yang, N., Braun, M., & O'Connor, R. (2001). Is reading important in reading-readiness program? A randomized field trial with teachers as program implementers. *Journal of Educational Psychology, 93,* 251–267.

Fuchs, L. S. (1993). Enhancing instructional programming and student achievement with curriculum-based measurement. In J. J. Kramer (Ed.), *Curriculum-based assessment* (pp. 65–104). Lincoln: Buros Institute of Mental Measurements, University of Nebraska.

Fuchs, L. S., & Deno, S. L. (1991). Paradigmatic distinctions between instructionally relevant measurement models. *Exceptional Children, 57,* 488–501.

Fuchs, L. S., & Deno, S. L. (1992). Effects of curriculum within curriculum-based measurement. *Exceptional Children, 58,* 232–243.

Fuchs, L. S., Deno, S. L., & Marston, D. (1983). Improving the reliability of curriculum-based measures of academic skills for psychoeducational decision making. *Diagnostique, 8,* 135–149.

Fuchs, L. S., Deno, S. L., & Mirkin, P. K. (1984). The effects of frequent curriculum-based measurement and evaluation on student achievement, pedagogy, and student awareness of learning. *American Educational Research Journal, 21,* 449–460.

Fuchs, L. S., & Fuchs, D. (1992). Identifying a measure for monitoring student reading progress. *School Psychology Review, 21,* 45–58.

Fuchs, L. S., & Fuchs, D. (1998). Curriculum-based measurement: A unifying framework for conceptualizing learning disability. *Learning Disability Research and Practice, 13,* 204–219.

Fuchs, L. S., & Fuchs, D. (1999). Monitoring student progress toward the development of reading competence: A review of three forms of classroom-based assessment. *School Psychology Review, 28,* 659–671.

Fuchs, L. S., Fuchs, D., & Deno, S. L. (1982). Reliability and validity of curriculum-based informal reading inventories. *Reading Research Quarterly, 18,* 6–26.

Fuchs, L. S., Fuchs, D., & Hamlett, C. L. (1989a). Effects of alternative goal structures within curriculum-based measurement. *Exceptional Children, 55,* 429–438.

Fuchs, L. S., Fuchs, D., & Hamlett, C. L. (1989b). Effects of instrumental use of curriculum-based measurement to enhance instructional programs. *Remedial and Special Education, 10*(2), 43–52.

Fuchs, L. S., Fuchs, D., & Hamlett, C. L. (1989c). Monitoring reading growth using student recalls: Effects of two teacher feedback systems. *Journal of Educational Research, 83,* 103–111.

Fuchs, L. S., Fuchs, D., Hamlett, C. L., & Allinder, R. M. (1989). The reliability and validity of skills analysis within curriculum-based measurement. *Diagnostique, 14,* 203–221.

Fuchs, L. S., Fuchs, D., Hamlett, C. L., & Allinder, R. M. (1991a). Effects of expert system advice within curriculum-based measurement on teacher planning and student achievement in spelling. *School Psychology Review, 20,* 49–66.

Fuchs, L. S., Fuchs, D., Hamlett, C. L., & Ferguson, C. (1992). Effects of expert system consultation within curriculum-based measurement using a reading maze task. *Exceptional Children, 58,* 436–450.

Fuchs, L. S., Fuchs, D., Hamlett, C. L., Phillips, N. B., & Bentz, J. (1994). Classwide curriculum-based measurement: Helping general educators meet the challenge of student diversity. *Exceptional Children, 60,* 518–537.

Fuchs, L. S., Fuchs, D., Hamlett, C. L., Phillips, N. B., & Karns, K. (1995). General educators' specialized adaptation for students with learning disabilities. *Exceptional Children, 61,* 440–459.

Fuchs, L. S., Fuchs, D., Hamlett, C. L., Phillips, N., Karns, K., & Dutka, S. (1997). Enhancing students' helping behavior during peer-mediated instruction with conceptual mathematics explanations. *Elementary School Journal, 97,* 223–250.

Fuchs, L.S., Fuchs, D., Hamlett, C. L., & Stecker, P. M. (1991). Effects of curriculum-based measurement and consultation on teacher planning and student achievement in mathematics operations. *American Educational Research Journal, 28,* 617–641.

Fuchs, L. S., Fuchs, D., Hamlett, C. L., Thompson, A., Roberts, P. H., Kubec, P., & Stecker, P. M. (1994). Technical features of a mathematics concepts and applications curriculum-based measurement system. *Diagnostique, 19*(4), 23–49.

Fuchs, L. S., Fuchs, D., Hamlett, C. L., Walz, L., & Germann, G. (1993). Formative evaluation of academic progress: How much growth can we expect? *School Psychology Review, 22,* 27–48.

Fuchs, L. S., Fuchs, D., & Maxwell, L. (1988). The validity of informal reading comprehension measures. *Remedial and Special Education, 9*(2), 20–29.

Fuchs, L. S., & Hamlett, C. L. (1997). *Predictive validity of curriculum-based measurement with respect to the TerraNova.* Unpublished data.

Fuchs, L. S., Hosp, M., Fuchs, D., & Hamlett, C. L. (2001a). *Effects of diagnostic feedback within curriculum-based measurement.* Manuscript in preparation.

Fuchs, L. S., Hosp, M., Fuchs, D., & Hamlett, C. L. (2001b). *Psychometric features of the Peabody Phonics Inventory.* Unpublished manuscript.

Good, R. H., Deno, S. L., & Fuchs, L. S. (1995, February). *Modeling academic growth for students with and without disabilities.* Paper presented at the third annual Pacific Coast Research Conference, Laguna Beach, CA.

Good, R. H., & Shinn, M. R. (1990). Forecasting accuracy of slope estimates for reading curriculum-based measurement: Empirical evidence. *Behavioral Assessment, 12,* 179–194.

Hosp, M., & Fuchs, L. S. (2001). *Technical features of curriculum-based measurement's reading aloud task in the early grades.* Manuscript submitted for publication.

Jones, E. D., & Krouse, J. P. (1988). The effectiveness of data-based instruction by student teachers in classrooms for pupils with mild learning handicaps. *Teacher Education and Special Education, 11,* 9–19.

Marston, D. (1987–1988). The effectiveness of special education: A time-series analysis of reading performance in regular and special education settings. *The Journal of Special Education, 21*(4), 13–26.

Marston, D. (1989). Curriculum-based measurement: What is it and why do it? In M. R. Shinn (Eds.). *Curriculum-based measurement: Assessing special children* (pp. 18–78). New York: Guilford.

Marston, D., & Deno, S. L. (1981). *The reliability of simple, direct measures of written expression* (Research Report No. 50). Minneapolis: University of Minnesota Institute for Research on Learning Disabilities.

Marston, D., Fuchs, L. S., & Deno, S. L. (1986). Measuring pupil progress: A comparison of standardized achievement tests and curriculum-related measures. *Diagnostique, 11,* 71–90.

Marston, D., & Magnusson, D. (1988). Curriculum-based assessment: District-level implementation. In J. Graden, J. Zins, & M. Curtis (Eds.), *Alternative educational delivery systems: Enhancing instructional options for all students* (pp. 137–172). Washington, DC: National Association of School Psychologists.

Rosenfeld, R. G. (1982). Short stature. In M. Green and J. Haggerty (Eds.). *Ambulatory Pediatrics–IV.* Philadelphia: Saunders.

Shinn, M. R., Tindal, G., Spira, D., & Marston, D. (1987). Practice of learning disabilities as social policy. *Learning Disability Quarterly, 10,* 17–28.

Speece, D. L., & Case, L. P. (2001). Classification in context: An alternative approach to identifying early reading disability. *Journal of Educational Psychology, 93,* 735–749.

Speece, D. L., Molloy, D. E., & Case, L. P. (2000, February). *Toward validating a model of reading disability identification based on response to treatment.* Presented at the annual Pacific Coast Research Conference, La Jolla, CA.

Stecker, P. M., & Fuchs, L. S. (1999). Effecting superior achievement using curriculum-based measurement: The importance of individual progress monitoring. *Learning Disabilities Research and Practice, 15,* 128–134.

Tanner, J. M., & Davies, P. S. W. (1985). Clinical longitudinal standards for height and weight velocity for North American children. *Journal of Pediatrics, 107,* 317.

Wesson, C. L. (1991). Curriculum-based measurement and two models of follow-up consultation. *Exceptional Children, 57,* 246–257.

Wesson, C. L., Skiba, R., Sevcik, B., King, R., & Deno, S. (1984). The effects of technically adequate instructional data on achievement. *Remedial and Special Education, 5,* 17–22.

Willett, J. B., Ayoub, C. C., & Robinson, D. (1991). Using growth modeling to examine systematic differences in growth: An example of change in the functioning of families at risk of maladaptive parenting, child abuse, or neglect. *Journal of Consulting and Clinical Psychology, 59,* 38–47.

Wolraich, M. (Ed.). (1996). *Disorders of development and training: A practical guide to assessment and management* (2nd ed.). St. Louis: Mosby.

PEABODY JOURNAL OF EDUCATION, 77(2), 85–105
Copyright © 2002, Lawrence Erlbaum Associates, Inc.

Assessment of Behavioral and Emotional Difficulties in Children and Adolescents

Sabine A. Wingenfeld
La Trobe University / Austin and Repatriation Medical Centre

Student behavioral and emotional difficulties, often comorbid with each other and with learning difficulties and academic underachievement, have become an increasing concern to educational settings. This article first provides a conceptual framework for child assessment and highlights the role of behavior rating scales and personality inventories. This article reviews the role of behavior rating scales and personality inventories as a tool for screening students whose behavioral and emotional difficulties may affect their learning, their interpersonal relationships at school, and students who may pose significant management problems for teachers. The utility of specific uni- and multidimensional scales is reviewed relative to major behavioral and emotional difficulties shown by school students. Issues with using these tools are discussed. The Student Behavior Survey (SBS), a teacher-report scale, is described to illustrate the relative contributions of these scales.

Teachers and schools are faced increasingly with mental health issues in their students. Mental health problems in children and adolescents are relatively common, affecting 14–20% of youths (Mash & Dozois, 1996; Roberts, Attkisson, & Rosenblatt, 1998; Sawyer et al., 2001), although estimates have varied due to differences in diagnostic conceptualization and methodology.

Requests for reprints should be sent to Sabine Wingenfeld, School of Psychological Science, La Trobe University VIC 3086, Australia.

Moreover, approximately 8–10% of youths are having problems of a severe nature, and 34.4% of children show only marginal adjustment and may be at risk for more severe problems later (Mash & Dozois, 1996).

For an average-sized classroom, these estimates translate into 3–5 students with some type of developmental or mental health problem, 1–2 students with serious psychopathology, and 8–10 students at risk for developing problems and possibly performing below their potential. Only about 25% of youths with behavior and emotional problems are obtaining professional help (Sawyer et al., 2001).

In response to increasing concerns about addressing student mental health needs, many schools and school systems have begun to implement approaches to mental health promotion and prevention of mental health problems in school-age children (for reviews, see Adelman & Taylor, 1999; Pfeiffer & Reddy, 1998; Wells, 2000). Expanded school mental health services incorporate a range of assessment, treatment, and consultation services (Flaherty & Weist, 1999). However, Adelman and Taylor (1999) have questioned whether schools have the resources to provide more than the "bare essentials" or to "even meet basic needs" (p. 140). Thus, children and adolescents with significant difficulties continue to challenge not only teachers but also school counselors and school psychologists, and they remain a considerable source of referrals to mental health facilities (Frick, Strauss, Lahey, & Christ, 1993).

This article focuses on issues in the identification and assessment of emotional and behavioral problems in children and adolescents. First, the need for an appropriate conceptual framework for understanding childhood disorders and the complexity of the assessment process for child and adolescent problems are highlighted, with special focus on the issue of comorbidity. Next, the role of objective behavior rating scales and questionnaires for the assessment process and issues in their use is briefly reviewed. In the final section, I describe the Student Behavior Survey (SBS) as an example of a teacher-report rating scale that can be helpful for obtaining systematic report on student adjustment at school.

Conceptual Framework

One legacy of my doctoral training at Peabody College is the importance of understanding children from a transactional–ecological viewpoint. Obviously, the developmental psychopathology viewpoint is by no means unique to Peabody College (Luthar, Burack, Cicchetti, &

Weisz, 1997; Mash & Dozois, 1996; Sameroff, Lewis, & Miller, 2000). Conceptualization of childhood disorders from this perspective implies understanding of emotional and behavioral adjustment within the context of child development, the interaction of the child with his or her environment, and the dynamic interplay of individual and systems variables over time. The developmental psychopathology perspective has been described as a macroparadigm that is superordinate to and complemented by a range of problem or disorder-specific theories (Luthar et al., 1997). From this perspective, childhood disorders cannot be easily attributed to a single or simple cause. Rather, various risk and protective factors interact to affect the current presentation and the future course of mental health problems. Different pathways can lead to similar outcomes (e.g., depression, equifinality) and similar initial pathways (e.g., exposure to trauma) that can lead to such diverse outcomes as adequate adjustment, mild depression, or severe anxiety (multifinality; Mash & Dozois, 1996). Assessment must be sensitive to developmental processes, especially the continuity and discontinuity of emotional and behavioral problems over time (Achenbach, 1997). Some behavior, though it may be concerning to teachers and disruptive in the classroom, may be seen best as reflecting a normal developmental stage that children will grow out of. Other problems (e.g., toileting problems) are most typical for certain age ranges and are not likely to persist. Certain mental health problems (e.g., conduct problems, inattention, and hyperactivity) remain stable over time although the exact nature of the concerns may change (Sanson & Prior, 1999). All these considerations make the identification and diagnosis of behavioral and emotional problems a complex process. In the assessment of children, a developmental psychopathology perspective requires obtaining and integrating information on a range of childhood and environmental factors. The theoretical notions of this approach also raise questions about the process of diagnosis and classification.

Diagnosis and Classification

Diagnosis and classification is often seen as a prerequisite to appropriate treatment. Two major systems for classification of childhood disorders are categorical systems (based on the presence or absence of symptoms or symptom clusters) such as the *Diagnostic and Statistical Manual of Mental Disorders* (American Psychiatric Association, 2000) and empirically based dimensional approaches. Dimensional systems are derived from multivariate psychological analyses of information provided by questionnaires and rating scales. The work by Achenbach (1997, 2000) exemplifies this approach. This research suggests that rather than a large number of distinct diagnostic categories, behavioral and emotional problems can be divided in several broad-band dimensions and several narrow-band dimensions within each broad-band factor. Extensive research has supported a broad-band externalizing dimension, consisting of disruptive behavior, and an internalizing dimension characterized by anxiety, depression, and somatic concerns. The controversy on whether categorical, dimensional, or integrated approaches provide the most valid understanding of children's mental health problems has been longstanding (Jensen & Hoagwood, 1997). This discussion is especially relevant with respect to the extensive co-occurrence of childhood disorders when using categorical classification systems.

Issue of Comorbidity

Many children and adolescents meet diagnostic criteria for more than one disorder (Angold, Costello, & Erkanli, 1999; Jensen, Martin, & Cantwell, 1997). One disorder characterized by extensive comorbidity is attention deficit hyperactivity disorder (ADHD). Szatmari, Offord, and Boyle (1989) found 44% of children with ADHD were likely to meet diagnostic criteria for one other disorder, while 32% of these children had at least two, and 11% at least three other disorders. The most common comorbid disorders are oppositional defiant disorder (ODD) and conduct disorder (CD), with up to 67% of children with ADHD meeting ODD criteria and 20% to 56% meeting criteria for CD (August, Realmuto, MacDonald, Nugent, & Crosby, 1996; Barkley, 1998). Comorbid ADHD and CD may be a distinct and more severe diagnostic entity (Gresham, Lane, & Lambros, 2000), with different neurocognitive test profiles (Clark, Prior, & Kinsella, 2000) and increased risk for negative developmental outcomes (MacDonald & Achenbach, 1996). The presence of learning disabilities can further complicate this picture. Estimates of comorbidity of ADHD with disorders of reading, written language, and mathematics have ranged from 15% to 60% (Barkley, 1998; Mayes, Calhoun, & Crowell, 2000). Research suggests distinct comorbid patterns between reading disorder and ADHD subtypes, possibly attributable to different genetic etiologies (Willcutt & Pennington, 2000).

Like ADHD, depression appears to be comorbid with a range of other disorders including anxiety (Brady & Kendall, 1992; Kessler, Avenevoli, & Merikangas, 2001), ADHD, ODD, and CD (e.g., McConaughy & Skiba, 1993; Meller & Borchardt, 1996; Rey, 1994).

The high comorbidity has several implications for the understanding, assessment, and treatment of childhood mental health problems. First, much research based on categorical models has examined individual disorders, not comorbid patterns, whereas many students, possibly those that are the most challenging in the school context, are likely to experience multiple difficulties. We need to develop and test conceptual models that help account for comorbidity (Jensen et al., 1997). Research is needed to examine whether childhood mental health problems are best understood as multiple homogeneous disorders or as comorbid subgroups. In addition, this research needs to link assessment to treatment. While mental health professionals may focus on diagnostic entities and taxonomies, teachers and school personnel may be more concerned about the functional impairments resulting from these problems and what to do about them. There are children who meet diagnostic criteria but show no functional impairments at home or at school (Shaffer, Fisher, & Lucas, 1999). With respect to ADHD, Pelham (2001) has raised the issue of how well diagnostic classification, or knowing that a child meets diagnostic criteria for a disorder (e.g., ADHD), informs intervention and treatment.

Second, the extensive comorbidity of externalizing and internalizing problems raises questions whether all difficulties experienced by a child are likely to be noticed equally. In the school setting, internalizing disorders can be difficult to detect because symptoms impact less obviously on others in the child's environment (Kamphaus & Frick, 1996). Hyperactivity, impulsive behavior, defiance, and aggression are more salient in the school context because such behavior can be strongly disruptive to the classroom. Co-occurring depression or anxiety may be overlooked in the presence of aggression or rule violations.

Third, comorbidity has implications for assessment practice. Initial screenings using parent, youth, or teacher report should use multidimensional measures to obtain an understanding of all the possible issues affecting the child. A unidimensional measure such as an ADHD screening tool can adequately identify inattention and hyperactivity or suggest the absence of ADHD. However, additional problems requiring more intensive interventions may be overlooked. Possible depression or anxiety that can make a child look inattentive at school may not be identified.

Complexity of the Assessment Process

The process of identifying whether a student shows symptoms of emotional and behavioral problems, whether these symptoms lead to some type of functional impairment at home, school, or in peer relations, and what interventions are indicated can be complicated. Depending on the nature of the concerns, parents, teachers, and the youth may hold discrepant opinions on (a) whether a problems exists and (b) the nature and severity of the problem (Duhig, Renk, Epstein, & Phares, 2000; Youngstrom, Loeber, & Stouthamer-Loeber, 2000).

The assessment process is complicated by the absence of gold standard assessment measures. Rather, multiple sources and multiple methods are combined to obtain a meaningful understanding of a student's learning ability and behavioral and emotional adjustment. Typical methods include clinical interviews, behavior observation, behavior rating scales, and psychological testing. All methods make unique contributions to this understanding and have their own shortcomings. Intelligence, achievement, neuropsychological, laboratory tests, and other performance-based measures are very helpful means of understanding a child's neurocognitive profile and academic progress. These measures, however, have often been found to have insufficient specificity, sensitivity, and predictive power for diagnosis of behavioral and emotional problems and for treatment planning (Frick, 2000). Among interview methods, structured diagnostic interviews (Shaffer et al., 1999) are likely to play an increasing role for DSM–IV-based diagnoses. These interviews are highly scripted to increase reliability and ease of administration and to minimize interviewer biases. Shaffer et al. suggested that computerized self-administered versions of these interviews can also serve as tools for large-scale screening in the schools. Structured, systematic observation of child behavior (Sattler, 2002) is useful for understanding the extent and severity of observable problem behavior, especially at school (McMahon & Estes, 1997), but less helpful for covert problem behavior or internalizing states such as depression.

Among the different assessment methods, objective behavior rating scales are the most common form of measurement of childhood psychopathology (Barkley, 1998). Rating scales are easy to administer, inexpensive, accurate, and allow for systematic comparison across informants (e.g., Barkley, 1998; Elliott, Busse, & Gresham, 1993; Lachar, 1998; Mash & Terdal, 1997). Objective rating scales, completed by parents, teachers, and the youths themselves, can (a) provide a cost-efficient tool for screening and identifying those students in need of further and more comprehensive evaluation, (b) assist the diagnostic process in helping to understand the extent and severity of student problems, (c) inform planning of interventions, and (d) measure response to school and clinic-based mental health and other interventions.

Types of Behavior Rating Scales

Parent, Teacher, and Self-Report

Parents, teachers, and the youths themselves make unique contributions to the identification and understanding of children's behavioral and emotional adjustment. Parent and teacher report is vital for young or developmentally delayed children who may lack the cognitive and linguistic capacity, reading skills, or persistence to complete a rating scale (Lachar, 1998). Moreover, younger children may show limited insight into the problematic nature of their behavior, especially if the behavior is disruptive and annoying to their parents, teachers, or peers. Self-report is highly desirable for older children and adolescents, especially when the concerns are about feelings (e.g., hopeless, worthless) and behaviors (e.g., theft) that are difficult to observe directly. Parent report contributes unique information on the child's development, relationships with family and with peers, and behavior in a range of diverse settings. Teachers, especially in elementary school, spend a large part of the day with the children (Sharpley, James, & Mavroudis, 1993). They observe children both in the highly structured, task-oriented classroom setting and in unstructured situations such as recess and play with peers (Epkins, 1995). Teachers are familiar with the age-appropriateness of children's academic status, attitude toward learning, peer relations, and behavior. At the secondary school level, when teachers have less contact with children than in the early school years, teacher report may be less accurate and youth self-report the most appropriate indicator of the student's feelings and behavior. These unique perspectives, while enriching the information obtained on a child, also create difficulty in integrating potentially discrepant information (Achenbach, McConaughy, & Howell, 1987; Stanger & Lewis, 1993).

Integrating information across informants. Concerns about agreement among respondents to behavior rating scales have been extensively explored (e.g., Duhig et al., 2000) since a seminal review paper on the issue by Achenbach et al. (1987). Poor agreement among informants has been attributed to a range of different reasons (Lachar, 1998; Wingenfeld, Lachar, Wrobel, & Gruber, 1998b).

1. Differences in child behavior across settings. Differences in expectations, structure, and parent/teacher skill in behavior management at

home and at school have been a principal explanation for rater discrepancies (Achenbach et al., 1987; Kamphaus & Frick, 1996).

2. Differences in scales used in assessment. Discrepancies between respondents may be due to differences in scale construction and validation. Scales vary in item content and in the accuracy of description of the target behavior (e.g., inattentive, absent-minded, or daydreaming). Measures differ in the scaling format: items may be rated as true or false, or on a multipoint rating scale that again may differ in asking about frequency of a behavior or whether the item is applicable to the child. Norms may differ in representativeness relative to the population census, and in breakdown by child age or by sex. Measures also differ in psychometric properties: internal consistency, test–retest reliability, and validity (Frick & Kamphaus, 2001). Many of these measures have been shown to have good convergent and construct validity but poor discriminant validity.

3. Differences in respondent perceptions. Depending on whether the problem is principally disruptive or internalizing, parents and teachers have been found to view behavior as more problematic than children (Duhig et al., 2000; Stanger & Lewis, 1993; Youngstrom et al., 2000). This raises the question on whether there is a best respondent for different problems at different ages and the rater's relevant contact with the child. Research has also called attention to the extensive role of mothers as the main parent-respondent (Phares, 1996) but more research is needed about agreement by both parents or the extent to which mothers and fathers rate behavior differently (Van der Valk, Van den Oord, Verhulst, & Boosma, 2001). Research on the influence of parental psychopathology, especially maternal depression, has shown short-and longterm effects on children's adjustment (Beardslee, Versage, & Gladstone, 1998) but remains equivocal on whether parents with their own mental health issues report more negative views of their off-spring (Richters, 1992; Youngstrom et al., 2000). Little research has addressed such issues in teachers. For example, little is known whether overworked and overwhelmed teachers have more negative views of students, and whether experience with behavior management or familiarity with the student (Ines & Sacco, 1992) may influence ratings.

4. Response sets and response styles. The effects of rater errors, response sets, and response styles are well documented in the adult assessment literature (e.g., Rogers, 1997). Lack of motivation or compliance may lead to an inconsistent or random response style, informants may not want to admit to mental health issues or may exaggerate the true nature of their problem. There has been, however, little systematic research on response styles in youths (Wrobel et al., 1999) or parents (Wingenfeld, Wrobel, Lachar, Gruber, & Pisecco, 2002) or teachers (Abikoff,

Courtney, Pelham, & Koplewicz, 1993) describing youths. Most measures of child and adolescent adjustment do not include scales to detect inconsistent, defensive, or exaggerated responding.

Unidimensional and Multidimensional Scales

Most inventories differ in the range of areas of adjustment they address. Some scales or sets of scales only address a single domain or dimension, such as attention problems or depression, whereas other scales include items in several areas.

Unidimensional scales.   Disorder or problem-specific scales have been developed for a wide range of areas. These scales can be disorder-specific (e.g., ADHD; Barkley, 1998; Conners, 1997; DuPaul et al., 1998) and problem-specific (e.g., social skills, executive function deficits; Gioia, Isquith, Guy, & Kenworthy, 2000). The measures vary in their conceptual bases, breadth, specificity to the problem, and psychometric properties. Scales for assessing internalizing problems such as depression (Sitenarios & Kovacs, 1999) or anxiety (Barrios & Hartmann, 1997) rely on self-report by the child or adolescent and often have no parent or teacher versions. For externalizing problems, report is typically provided by parents or teachers.

Multidimensional scales.   Multidimensional rating scales concern child status in several domains of adjustment. Many of these scales contain specific areas of adjustment (e.g., attention, social problems, anxiety, or depression) and broad areas of adjustment such as an externalizing dimension, consisting of disruptive behavior, and an internalizing dimension characterized by anxiety, depression, somatic concerns. Multidimensional scales allow screening for the presence of a specific problem and of comorbid conditions, as well as for the absence of problems (Lachar, 1998).

A recent development is the construction of sets of measures that sample multiple domains and include forms for parents, teachers, and self-report for older children and adolescents (Kline, 1994, 1995). Compared to unidimensional measures developed by different researchers, integrated sets of measures offer several advantages, including greater similarity of item content and format and overlapping normative samples (Wingenfeld, Lachar, Gruber, & Kline, 1998a). This may also enhance comparison of scores from different informants.

The earliest set of multidimensional multisource measures are the parent–informant Child Behavior Checklist, the Teacher Report Form, and the Youth Self-Report questionnaires developed by Achenbach (see Achenbach, 1999, for a recent review). Another set of multi-informant questionnaires is the Behavior Assessment System for Children (Reynolds & Kamphaus, 1992), which consists of the parent rating scale, the teacher rating scale, and the self-report of personality. A third set is the Conners' Parent and Teacher Rating Scales (Conners, 1997). The 1997 revision now includes a youth self-report form. A fourth set comprises the second edition of the Personality Inventory for Children (PIC–2; Lachar & Gruber, 2002), the Personality Inventory for Youth (PIY; Lachar & Gruber, 1995a, 1995b) and the Student Behavior Survey (SBS; Lachar, Wingenfeld, Kline, & Gruber, 2000). These sets of measures and their relative advantages and shortcomings have been extensively described in recent literature (Frick & Kamphaus, 2001; Lachar, 1998, 1999; Sattler, 2002; Shapiro & Kratochwill, 2000). The remainder of this article therefore focuses on the teacher-report SBS as a tool for identifying and formulating hypotheses about students' emotional and behavioral adjustment.

The Student Behavior Survey

In 1992, David Lachar, Rex Kline, Chris Gruber, and I began to develop a teacher rating scale that would serve both as a stand-alone instrument and as a complement to the PIC–2 (Lachar & Gruber, 2002) and the self-report PIY (Lachar & Gruber, 1995a, 1995b). Different from other rating scales, we did not emphasize equivalence of item content for parent and teacher report in the development of the SBS. Rather, we focused on those behaviors that were identified in the literature as most relevant for the school context and rated reliably by teachers. This test development process resulted in 102 items of which 58 refer specifically to in-class or in-school behaviors. Different from other teacher rating scales, items are not presented in random order but are organized under meaningful headings describing the content of 11 of the 14 dimensions assessed in the SBS. The SBS takes approximately 10 min to complete. In the initial validation studies, the vast majority of teachers rated the length of the SBS as appropriate.

The SBS consists of three major sections (see Table 1 for scales and sample items). The first section, academic resources, includes four dimensions that focus on student strengths. The academic performance scales ask teachers to rate eight areas of student achievement such as reading, maths, and oral expression on a five-point scale (*deficient, below average, average, above average, superior*). The next three dimensions are rated on a four-point scale *(never, seldom, sometimes, often)*, and items are worded positively to denote competencies. Academic habits examines student motivation, persistence, and approach to learning. Social skills addresses attention to social cues and collaborative relationships with peers. The parent participation scale taps into parental expectations, encouragement of their child's learning, and collaborative relationship with the school.

Table 1

Domains Assessed by the Student Behavior Survey

SBS Scale	Number of Items	Interpret as Weakness: Scores of	Sample Items Representing SBS Domains
Academic performance (AP)	8	≤ 40 T	Reading comprehension Mathematics
Academic habits (AH)	13	≤ 40 T	Completes homework assignments Waits for his/her turn
Social skills (SS)	8	≤ 40 T	Helps other students Works cooperatively with other students
Parent participation (PP)	6	≤ 40 T	Parents meet with school staff when asked Parents encourage achievement
Health concerns (HC)	6	≥ 60 T	Complains of headaches Talks about being sick
Emotional distress (ED)	15	≥ 60 T	Appears moody or too serious Expects to fail or do poorly
Unusual behavior (UB)	7	≥ 60 T	Behavior is strange and peculiar Confused by what other people say
Social problems (SP)	12	≥ 60 T	Avoids social interaction in class Ignored/rejected by other students
Verbal aggression (VA)	7	≥ 60 T	Insults other students Threatens other students
Physical aggression (PA)	5	≥ 60 T	Destroys property when angry Hits or pushes other students
Behavior problems (BP)	15	≥ 60 T	Disrupts class by misbehaving Steals from others
Attention deficit hyperactivity (ADH)	16	≥ 60 T	Impulsive; acts without thinking
Oppositional defiant (OPD)	16	≥ 60 T	Disobeys class or school rules
Conduct problems (CP)	16	≥ 60 T	Lies to school personnel

The second SBS section, adjustment problems, includes seven areas of concern about student adjustment. Items in this section are also rated on a four-point scale (*never, seldom, sometimes, often*) but are worded negatively. The health concerns scale describes children who appear tired and complain of sickness and aches. The emotional distress scale includes items on anxiety, fear, and worry, as well as items on negative mood and low self-confidence. Unusual behavior refers to students showing behavior that teachers would see as strange, odd, or peculiar. The social problems scale includes items that address social discomfort and disconnectedness from others as well as behavior that angers others. Item content on the verbal aggression scale includes argumentativeness, talking back, teasing, insults, and verbal threats. The physical aggression scale describes students who hit, fight, destroy property, or attempt to hurt others. Items on the behavior problems scale refer to a range of disruptive behaviors such as impulsive and hyperactive behavior, disruptiveness, defiance, disobedience, and rule violations.

The third SBS section, disruptive behavior, consists of three 16-item, nonoverlapping scales that were constructed from 48 SBS items that describe behavior consistent with DSM–IV diagnoses of ADHD, ODD, and CD. The development and validation of these scales is described by Pisecco et al. (1999).

For all scales, raw scores are converted to linear T-scores. As shown in Table 1, for the academic resources section scores equal to or less than 40 T denote weaknesses, whereas the adjustment problems and disruptive behavior provide two interpretive ranges for behavioral and emotional concerns: scores of 60 to 69 T and 70 T or above.

The SBS is based on a large nationally representative (USA) regular education sample ($N = 2,612$) and a clinically and educationally referred sample ($N = 1,315$). Initial analyses (Wingenfeld et al., 1998a) supported gender and age-based (5–11 and 12–18 years) norms. The SBS scales demonstrate high internal consistencies both for the regular education (median alpha = .89) and the clinically and educationally referred sample (median alpha = .89). Median test–retest reliabilities are .86 for a short test–retest interval and .71 for an 11.4 to 28.5 week period. The median interrater reliability is .73 (Lachar et al., 2000).

The SBS shows good construct validity as items correlate meaningfully with the dimensions in which they have been placed. Factor analysis provides support for a three-factor solution for referred samples. SBS results also correlated meaningfully with clinician, parent, student self-report, and teacher ratings. In validation studies, the SBS was found to discriminate between students with disruptive and nondisruptive problems. Furthermore, using special education definitions, meaningful group differences were obtained between children with intellectual disabilities, emotional impairments, and learning disabilities (Lachar et al., 2000; Pisecco et al., 1999; Wingenfeld et al., 1998a). These analyses suggest that the SBS has the necessary psychometric properties for educational and clinical applications.

In the final section of this article, I illustrate the inferential process of generating hypotheses about student adjustment and integrating other information for diagnostic purposes based on SBS results.

Generating Hypotheses About Child Adjustment Based on SBS Profiles

Concerns About Academic Achievement and Emotional Adjustment

Three SBS scales are meaningfully elevated in the profiles shown in Figure 1: The low score on academic problems (AP) could suggest a specific learning disability, overall lower intellectual ability underachievement due to emotional distress. Comparison to the academic habits (AH)

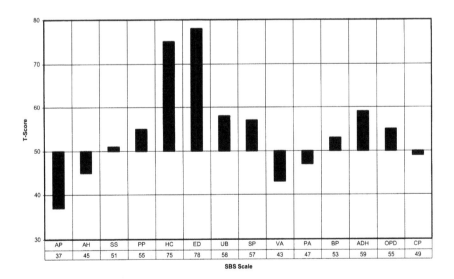

Figure 1. Concerns about academic achievement and emotional adjustment.
  Note: For scales AP, AH, SS, and PP, scores equal to or less than 40 T denote problems; for scales HC to CP, scores of 60 T or higher denote some difficulty, with scores at or above 70 T indicating increasing severity.

scale (in the nonproblematic range), suggests a young person who is struggling academically despite adequate effort and learning habits. Inspection of individual items on scale AP can help with hypotheses on the presence of a learning disorder: consistent endorsement of items across the eight areas of academic achievement might suggest overall lower ability, whereas scatter (e.g., deficient performance in maths, and average performance in the other areas) may indicate specific learning disability. Obviously, to support either hypothesis an evaluation using the other assessment methods described in this special issue is needed.

The other two elevated scales are health concerns (HC) and emotional distress (ED), suggesting that this student presents in school as anxious, worried, and depressed and may make health complaints. With respect to the elevated scores on the HC and ED, inspection of individual items can suggest directions for further evaluation. Follow-up administration of the multidimensional PIC–2 and the PIY to obtain parent and youth report for comparison with teacher report is one possible step. Use of single domain ratings scales such as the Children's Depression Inventory or a clinical interview (Sattler, 1998) may help to clarify the severity of depressive symptoms. These additional measures can then clarify to what extent this child's behavior at home may be different from at school: all the remaining SBS scales are in the nonclinical range, suggesting that the teacher noted no disruptive or other problem behavior.

Comorbid Externalizing and Internalizing Problems

Figure 2 demonstrates another SBS pattern, not unusual for elementary school-age boys referred to an outpatient child and adolescent mental health service. First, teacher report suggests presence of multiple concerns; of the 14 scales, only 3 are not elevated. It is interesting to note that this child shows average achievement at school (AP) despite poor learning habits and motivation (AH). This pattern could suggest that the extensive emotional and behavioral issues in this child's life do not appear to affect his performance. Alternatively, this child may be intellectually gifted and underachieving relative to his potential. A cognitive evaluation can clarify this hypothesis. Hypothesis generation with this profile could also be approached by looking at the disruptive behavior scales first: elevations suggest comorbid ADHD and ODD, as well as poor social skills (SS) and social problems (SP). Verbal and physical aggression may contribute to social difficulty and peer rejection. This child is also showing moderate anxiety and depression. The elevation of the unusual behavior (UB) scale, together with the social scales (SS and SP), raises a further

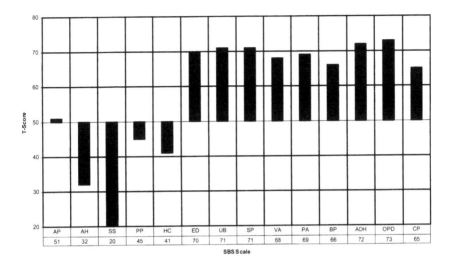

Figure 2. Comorbid externalizing and internalizing problems.

hypothesis to explore: the possibility that the child, though of average cognitive ability, has a pervasive developmental problem that is contributing to the behavioral concerns. This figure also illustrates the importance of multidimensional screening, and when multiple concerns are evident, the need for a comprehensive evaluation.

Rater Agreement on Problem Behavior

Figure 3 illustrates the issue of teacher agreement. In this case, the classroom teacher, the behavioral support teacher, and the counselor separately completed the SBS of a third-grade boy who showed severe aggression, noncompliance, and rule violations. All respondents reported that this child was one of the most challenging they had encountered in their teaching careers. At the time of this evaluation, expulsion from regular school was being considered. In general, informants are in agreement that this child has serious conduct problems, manifesting through verbal aggression (verbal threats, swearing, insulting of peers) and physical aggression (attempts to hurt peers seriously). The discrepancy of views on physical aggression is noteworthy. The support teacher was working one-on-one with this child and did not observe the physical fights he initiated with peers. This profile also illustrates the extent of this child's problems and needs. In addition to concerns about his serious rule violations and defiance, results suggest inattention and hyperactivity, poor social skills and

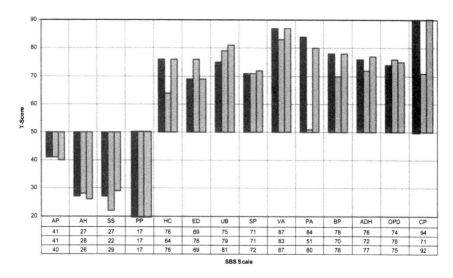

SBS Scale	AP	AH	SS	PP	HC	ED	UB	SP	VA	PA	BP	ADH	OPD	CP
	41	27	27	17	76	69	75	71	87	84	78	76	74	94
	41	28	22	17	64	76	79	71	83	51	70	72	76	71
	40	26	29	17	76	69	81	72	87	80	78	77	75	92

Figure 3. Rater agreement on problem behavior.

Note: First bar = regular classroom teacher; Second bar = support teacher; Third bar = counselor. For scales AP, AH, SS, and PP, scores equal to or less than 40 T denote problems; for scales HC to CP, scores of 60 T or higher denote some difficulty, with scores at or above 70 T indicating increasing severity.

peer relationship problems, health concerns, and emotional distress. Teachers saw this child's behavior as very strange. The low parent participation score is also noteworthy; it suggests parents with unrealistic expectations and attitudes toward the school and that parents and teachers were not working together effectively to help this child. This profile also illustrates another important point: Could the classroom teacher have been exaggerating this child's problems? The teacher's verbal report of "worst child encountered in my teaching career" is supported by the high SBS elevations and the corroborating SBS results of the other two respondents.

The figures provided here were treated as a first step in the investigative process of determining the presence and severity of behavioral and emotional problems in school-age children. The hypotheses generated by such profiles need to be corroborated with other assessment methods to obtain a meaningful understanding of a child's adjustment and to determine appropriate interventions both within the school and from mental health services.

Conclusion

While multimethod, multisource assessment is a desirable goal for understanding learning, behavioral, and emotional concerns in students, comprehensive evaluations are also costly. Multidimensional behavior rating scales, especially those that are part of a set of parent, teacher, and self-report measures, are an efficient, reliable, and valid means of identifying students in need and issues in their adjustment at school. Teacher rating scales, such as the SBS, can generate hypotheses before or in the early stages of an educational or clinical evaluation. Multidimensional scales can help to identify the range of potential comorbid problems a student may experience. Measures that include scales on academic achievement and habits can suggest hypotheses about a student's learning as well as his or her behavioral or emotional adjustment. These hypotheses can then be further explored with multidimensional parent and self-report questionnaires, and more in-depth cognitive, achievement, neuropsychological, and other psychometric procedures.

References

Abikoff, H., Courtney, M., Pelham, W. E., & Koplewicz, H. S. (1993). Teachers' ratings of disruptive behaviors: The influence of halo effects. *Journal of Abnormal Child Psychology, 21,* 519–533.

Achenbach, T. M. (1999). The Child Behavior Checklist and related instruments. In M. E. Maruish (Ed.), *The use of psychological testing for treatment planning and outcome assessment* (2nd ed., pp. 429–466). Mahwah, NJ: Lawrence Erlbaum Associates, Inc.

Achenbach, T. M. (1997). What is normal? What is abnormal? Developmental perspectives on behavioral and emotional problems. In S. S. Luthar, J. A. Burack, D. Cicchetti, & J. R. Weisz (Eds.), *Developmental psychopathology: Perspectives on adjustment, risk, and disorders* (pp. 93–114). New York: Cambridge University Press.

Achenbach, T. M. (2000). Assessment of psychopathology. In A. J. Sameroff & M. Lewis (Eds.), *Handbook of developmental psychopathology* (2nd ed., pp. 41–56). New York: Kluwer Academic/Plenum.

Achenbach, T. M., McConaughy, S. H., & Howell, C. T. (1987). Child/adolescent behavioral and emotional problems: Implications of cross-informant correlations for situational specificity. *Psychological Bulletin, 101,* 213–232.

Adelman, H. S., & Taylor, L. (1999). Mental health in schools and systems restructuring. *Clinical Psychology Review, 2,* 137–163.

American Psychiatric Association. (2000). *Diagnostic and statistical manual for mental disorders* (4th ed., rev., DSM–IV–TR). Washington, DC: Author.

Angold, A., Costello, E. J., & Erkanli, A. (1999). Comorbidity. *Journal of Child Psychology & Psychiatry & Allied Disciplines, 40,* 57–87.

August, G. J., Realmuto, G. M., MacDonald, A. W., Nugent, S. M., & Crosby, R. (1996). Prevalence of ADHD in comorbid disorders among elementary school children screened for disruptive behavior. *Journal of Abnormal Child Psychology, 24,* 571–595.

Barkley, R. A. (1998). Attention-deficit hyperactivity disorder: A handbook for diagnosis and treatment (2nd ed.). New York: Guilford.

Barrios, B. A., & Hartmann, D. P. (1997). Fears and anxieties. In E. J. Mash & L. G. Terdal (Eds.), *Assessment of childhood disorders* (3rd ed., pp. 230–327). New York: Guilford.

Beardslee, W. R., Versage, E. M., & Gladstone, T. R. C. (1998). Children of affectively ill parents: A review of the past 10 years. *Journal of the American Academy of Child and Adolescent Psychiatry, 37,* 1134–1142.

Brady, E. U., & Kendall, P. C. (1992). Comorbidity of anxiety and depression in children and adolescents. *Psychological Bulletin, 111,* 244–255.

Clark, C., Prior, M., & Kinsella, G. J. (2000). Do executive function deficits differentiate between adolescents with ADHD and oppositional defiant disorder/conduct disorder? *Journal of Abnormal Child Psychology, 28,* 403–414.

Conners, C. K. (1997). *Conners' Rating Scale Manual–Revised: Technical Manual.* North Tonawanda, NY: Multi-Health Systems, Inc.

Duhig, A. M., Renk, K., Epstein, M. K., & Phares, V. (2000). Interparental agreement on internalizing, externalizing, and total behavior problems: A meta-analysis. *Clinical Psychology: Science and Practice, 7,* 435–453.

DuPaul, G. J., Power, T. J., Anastopoulos, A. D., Reid, R., McGoey, K., & Ikeda, M. (1998). Reliability and validity of teacher ratings of attention deficit/hyperactivity disorder symptoms. *Psychological Assessment, 16,* 55–68.

Elliott, S. N., Busse, R. T., & Gresham, F. M. (1993). Behavior rating scales: Issues of use and development. *School Psychology Review, 22,* 313–321.

Epkins, C. C. (1995). Teachers' ratings of inpatient children's depression, anxiety, and aggression: A preliminary comparison between inpatient-facility and community-based teachers' ratings and their correspondence with children's self-report. *Journal of Clinical Child Psychology, 24,* 63–70.

Flaherty, L. T., & Weist, M. D. (1999). School-based mental health services: The Baltimore models. *Psychology in the Schools, 36,* 379–389.

Frick, P. J. (Ed.). (2000). Special Section: Laboratory and performance-based measures of childhood disorders. *Journal of Clinical Child Psychology, 29,* 475–568.

Frick, P. J., & Kamphaus, R. W. (2001). Standardized rating scales in the assessment of children's emotional and behavioral problems. In E. G. Walker & M. C. Roberts (Eds.), *Handbook of clinical child psychology* (3rd ed., pp. 190–204). New York: Wiley.

Frick, P. J., Strauss, C. C., Lahey, B. B., & Christ, M. G. (1993). Behavior disorders of children. In P. B. Sutker & H. E. Adams (Eds.), *Comprehensive handbook of psychopathology* (2nd ed., pp. 765–789). New York: Plenum.

Gioia, G. A., Isquith, P. K., Guy, S. C., & Kenworthy, L. (2000). *BRIEF: Behavior rating of inventory of executive function.* Odessa, FL: Psychological Assessment Resources.

Gresham, F. M., Lane, K. L., & Lambros, K. (2000). Comorbidity of conduct problems and ADHD: Identification of fledgling psychopaths. *Journal of Emotional and Behavioral Disorders, 8,* 83–101.

Ines, T. M., & Sacco, W. P. (1992). Factors related to correspondence between teacher ratings of elementary student depression and student self-ratings. *Journal of Consulting and Clinical Psychology, 60,* 140–142.

Jensen, P. S., & Hoagwood, K. (1997). The book of names: DSM–IV in context. *Development and Psychopathology, 9,* 231–249.

Jensen, P. S., Martin, D., & Cantwell, D. P. (1997). Comorbidity in ADHD: Implications for research, practice and DSM–IV. *Journal of the American Academy of Child and Adolescent Psychiatry, 36,* 1065–1079.

Kamphaus, R. W., & Frick, P. J. (1996). Clinical assessment of child and adolescent personality and behavior. Neidham Heights, MA: Allyn & Bacon.

Kessler, R. C., Avenevoli, S., & Merikangas, K. R. (2001). Mood disorders in children and adolescents: An epidemiological perspective. *Biological Psychiatry, 49,* 1002–1014.

Kline, R. B. (1994). New objective rating scales for child assessment, I. Parent- and teacher-informant inventories: The Behavior Assessment System for Children, the Child Behavior Checklist, and the Teacher Report Form. *Journal of Psychoeducational Assessment, 12,* 289–306.

Kline, R. B. (1995). New objective rating scales for child assessment, II. Self-report scales: The Behavior Assessment System for Children, the Youth Self-Report, and the Personality Inventory for Youth. *Journal of Psychoeducational Assessment, 13,* 169–193.

Lachar, D. (1998). Observations of parents, teachers, and children: Contributions to the objective multidimensional assessment of youth. In A.S. Bellack & M. Hersen (Series Eds.), & C. R. Reynolds (Vol. Ed.), *Comprehensive clinical psychology: Vol. 4. Assessment* (pp. 371–401). New York: Pergamon.

Lachar, D. (1999). Personality Inventory for Children, Second Edition (PIC–2), Personality Inventory for Youth (PIY), and Student Behavior Survey (SBS). In M. E. Maruish (Ed.), *The use of psychological testing for treatment planning and outcome assessment* (2nd ed., pp. 399–427). Mahwah, NJ: Lawrence Erlbaum Associates, Inc.

Lachar, D., & Gruber, C. P. (1995a). *Personality Inventory for Youth (PIY) manual: Administration and interpretation guide.* Los Angeles: Western Psychological Services.

Lachar, D., & Gruber, C. P. (1995b). *Personality Inventory for Youth (PIY) technical guide.* Los Angeles: Western Psychological Services.

Lachar, D., & Gruber, C. P. (2002). *Personality Inventory for Children* (2nd ed., PIC–2). Los Angeles: Western Psychological Services.

Lachar, D., Wingenfeld, S. A., Kline, R. B., & Gruber, C. P. (2000). *Student Behavior Survey.* Los Angeles: Western Psychological Services.

Luthar, S. S., Burack, J. A., Cicchetti, D., & Weisz, J. R. (1997). *Developmental psychopathology: Perspectives on adjustment, risk, and disorders.* New York: Cambridge University Press.

MacDonald, V., & Achenbach, T. (1996). Attention problems versus conduct problems as six-year predictors of problem scores in a national sample. *Journal of the American Academy of Child and Adolescent Psychiatry, 35,* 1237–1246.

Mash, E. J., & Dozois, D. J. (1996). Child psychopathology: A developmental systems perspective. In E. J. Mash & A. Barkley (Eds.), *Child psychopathology* (pp. 3–60). New York: Guilford.

Mash, E. J., & Terdal, L. G. (1997). Assessment of child and family disturbance: A behavioral-systems approach. In E. J. Mash & L. G. Terdal (Eds.), *Assessment of childhood disorders* (3rd ed., pp. 3–68). New York: Guilford.

Mayes, S. D., Calhoun, S. L., & Crowell, E. W. (2000). Learning disabilities and ADHD: Overlapping spectrum disorders. *Journal of Learning Disabilities, 33,* 117–124.

McConaughy, S. H., & Skiba, R. J. (1993). Comorbidity of externalizing and internalizing problems. *School Psychology Review, 22,* 421–436.

McMahon, R. J. & Estes, A. M. (1997). Conduct problems. In E. J. Mash & L. G. Terdal (Eds.), *Assessment of childhood disorders* (3rd ed., pp. 130–193). New York: Guilford.

Meller, W.H., & Borchardt, C.M. (1996). Comorbidity of major depression and conduct disorder. *Journal of Affective Disorders, 39,* 123–126.

Pelham, W. E. (2001). Are ADHD/I and ADHD/C the same or different? Does it matter? *Clinical Psychology Science and Practice, 8,* 502–506.

Pfeiffer, S. I., & Reddy, L. A. (1998). School-based mental health programs in the United States: Present status and a blueprint for the future. *School Psychology Review, 27,* 84–96.

Phares, V. (1996). *Fathers and developmental psychopathology.* New York: Wiley.

Pisecco, S., Lachar, D., Gruber, C. P., Gallen, R. T., Kline, R. B., & Huzinec, C. (1999). Development and validation of disruptive behavior scales for the Student Behavior Survey (SBS). *Journal of Psychoeducational Assessment, 17,* 314–331.

Reynolds, C. R., & Kamphaus, R. W. (1992). *Behavior Assessment System for Children manual.* Circle Pines, MN: American Guidance Service.

Rey, J. M. (1994). Comorbidity between disruptive disorders and depression in referred adolescents. *Australian and New Zealand Journal of Psychiatry, 28,* 106–113.

Richters, J. E. (1992). Depressed mothers as informants about their children: A critical review of the evidence of distortion. *Psychological Bulletin, 112,* 485–499.

Roberts, R. E., Attkisson, C. C., & Rosenblatt, A. (1998). Prevalence of psychopathology among children and adolescents. *American Journal of Psychiatry, 155,* 715–725.

Rogers, R. (Ed.). (1997). *Clinical assessment of malingering and deception* (2nd ed.). New York: Guilford.

Sameroff, A. J., Lewis, M., & Miller, S. M. (Eds.). (2000). *Handbook of developmental psychopathology* (2nd ed.). New York: Kluwer Academic/Plenum.

Sanson, A., & Prior, M. (1999). Temperament and behavioral precursors to oppositional defiant disorder and conduct disorder. In C. Herbert, & A. E. Hogan (Eds.), *Handbook of disruptive behavior disorders* (pp. 397–417). New York: Plenum.

Sawyer, M. G., Arney, F. M., Baghurst, P. A., Clark, J. J., Graetz, B. W., Kosky, R. J., Nurcombe, B., et al. (2001). The mental health of young people in Australia: Key findings from the Child and Adolescent Component of the National Survey of Mental Health and Well-Being. *Australian and New Zealand Journal of Psychiatry, 35,* 806–814.

Sattler, J. M. (1998). *Clinical and forensic interviewing of children and families.* San Diego, CA: Jerome M. Sattler, Publisher.

Sattler, J. M. (2002). *Assessment of children: Behavioral and clinical applications.* San Diego, CA: Jerome M. Sattler, Publisher.

Shaffer, D., Fisher, P. W., & Lucas, C. P. (1999). Respondent-based interviews. In D. Shaffer, C. P. Lucas, & J. E. Richter (Eds.), *Diagnostic assessment in child and adolescent psychopathology* (pp. 3–33). New York: The Guilford.

Sharpley, C. F., James, A., & Mavroudis, A. (1993). Self-ratings versus teacher ratings of adolescents' type A behavior in the normal classroom. *Psychology in the Schools, 30,* 119–124.

Shapiro, E. S., & Kratochwill, T. R. (2000). Behavioral assessment in schools: Theory, research, and clinical foundations (2nd ed.). New York: The Guilford.

Sitarenios, G., & Kovacs, M. (1999). Use of the Children's Depression Inventory. In M. E. Maruish (Ed.), *The use of psychological testing for treatment planning and outcome assessment* (2nd ed., pp. 267–298). Hillsdale, NJ: Lawrence Erlbaum Associates, Inc.

Stanger, C., & Lewis, M. (1993). Agreement among parents, teachers, and children on internalizing and externalizing behavior problems. *Journal of Clinical Child Psychology, 22,* 107–115.

Szatmari, P., Offord, D. R., & Boyle, M. H. (1989). Ontario child health study: Prevalence of attention deficit disorder with hyperactivity. *Journal of Child Psychology and Psychiatry, 30,* 219–230.

Van der Valk, J. C., Van den Oord, E. J. C., Verhulst, F. C., & Boosma, D. I. (2001). Using parental ratings to study the etiology of 3-year-old twin's problem behaviors: Different views or rater bias? *Journal of Child Psychology & Psychiatry & Allied Disciplines, 42,* 921–931.

Wells, J. (2000). Promoting emotional well-being in schools. In A. Buchanan & B. Hudson (Eds.), *Promoting children's emotional well-being* (pp. 161–192). New York: Oxford University Press.

Willcutt, E. G., Pennington, B. F., & DeFries, J. C. (2000). Etiology of inattention and hyperactivity/impulsivity in a community sample of twins with learning difficulties. *Journal of Abnormal Child Psychology, 28,* 149–165.

Wingenfeld, S. A., Lachar, D., Gruber, C. P., & Kline, R. (1998a). Development of the teacher-informant Student Behavior Survey. *Journal of Psychoeducational Assessment, 16,* 226–249.

Wingenfeld, S. A., Lachar, D., Wrobel, T., & Gruber., C. P. (1998b, August). *Constructing scales to measure symptom exaggeration and malingering.* Paper presented at the 106th Annual Convention of the American Psychological Association, San Francisco.

Wingenfeld, S. A., Wrobel, T. A., Lachar, D., Gruber, C. P., & Pisecco, S. (2002) *Detecting malingering on the Personality Inventory for Children.* Manuscript submitted for publication.

Wrobel, T. A., Lachar, D., Wrobel, N. H., Morgan, S. T., Gruber, C. P., Neher, J. A. (1999). Performance of the Personality Inventory for Youth validity scales. *Assessment, 6,* 367–379.

Youngstrom, E., Loeber, R., & Stouthamer-Loeber, M. (2000). Patterns and correlates of agreement between parent, teacher, and male adolescent ratings of externalizing and internalizing problems. *Journal of Consulting and Clinical Psychology, 68,* 1038–1050.

PEABODY JOURNAL OF EDUCATION, 77(2), 106–116

Measurement and the Diagnosis and Treatment of Language Disorders in Children

Stephen Camarata

Hearing and Speech Science Department
Vanderbilt University

Keith E. Nelson

Penn State University

The accurate diagnosis of clinical conditions that include language disorders (e.g., developmental disabilities, autism, and specific language impairment) rests squarely on the accurate measurement of language and related abilities. In addition, because the goal of any treatment program is to generate measurable progress in language function, it is essential that treatment programs be designed within the context of state-of-the-art measurement. Therefore, both diagnosis and treatment of language disorders in children are founded on measurement. However, recent advances in the measurement of language abilities have outpaced changes in diagnostic classification and treatment methods. This should not imply that diagnosis be solely guided by available subtests on an intelligence battery or that treatment be designed primarily to teach the items used in measurement. Rather the goal should be to diagnose with an eye on the results of measurement and develop treatments that result in advances in the underlying skills that are sampled in the measurement procedures. Thus, the purpose of this article is to review the measurement of oral

Requests for reprints should be sent to Stephen M. Camarata, Hearing and Speech Science Department, Bill Wilkerson Center, Vanderbilt University, 1114 19th Ave. S., Nashville, TN 37212.

language in children and discuss methods for ensuring that diagnosis and treatment include consideration of these measures. In addition, the ways that treatment outcomes can ultimately inform diagnosis will be discussed.

Measurement is the foundation for the accurate diagnosis of disabling conditions and is also essential for determining whether a treatment has been effective. However, one could argue that there is a striking disparity in the application of state-of-the-art measurement procedures to the problems of differential diagnosis of conditions involving language disorders. Similarly, one could argue that many treatment programs are constructed and delivered with little, if any, consideration of measuring progress in a psychometrically sound manner. Perhaps this disparity arises in part because of the different views of language measurement among scientists and clinicians and the different models of language that are currently available. The purpose of this article is to review the measurement of oral language in children and discuss potential methods for applying these techniques to diagnosis and for ensuring that treatment includes consideration of these measures. In addition, the ways that measurement in treatment can ultimately inform diagnosis will be discussed.

What is language? What should be assessed when measuring language ability? The answers to these questions depend largely on one's background and orientation to measurement issues (Camarata, 1991). It is not surprising that cognitive scientists, educators, psychologists, linguists, and speech pathologists often have very different perspectives on what comprises language. These differing perspectives on language are reflected in the current plethora of language instruments available on the market and reported in the literature (Salvia & Ysseldyke, 1995), each with an apparently unique and oblique method of assessing language. As a result, the measurement of oral language can be rather elusive. Indeed, one could argue that certain kinds of tasks touted as oral language actually fall outside the construct; conversely, many language-free or performance measures actually are directly or indirectly dependent on language ability (cf. Camarata & Swisher, 1990). It is also important to bear in mind that theoretical perspectives on the nature of language have been changing dramatically over the past 3 decades and that an understanding of the neural aspects of language processing has also advanced significantly during this time. Similarly, the technology used to assess language has shadowed theoretical shifts and neurological advances (e.g., Merzenich, et al., 1996). Yet, new instruments do not displace established tests in the way that new theories replace older theoretical models. Although it can be argued that testing ultimately drives treatment methods, advances in measurement are not often included in treatment paradigms.

Defining Language

Perhaps the most straightforward way of defining language is to simply say that language is a code for conveying thoughts or ideas (Bloom & Lahey, 1978; Camarata, 1991). But this disarmingly simple description belies the myriad of cognitive skills that are believed to be employed in actually using language (Schrank, Flanagan, Woodcock, & Mascolo, 2002). This divergent perspective on language as a construct has had important ramifications for defining and measuring language. Language theorists have been interested in the descriptive aspects of language (e.g., Bloomfield, 1933). There also has been a long-standing interest in explanatory mechanisms (e.g., Miller, 1951; Osgood, 1971) that ultimately are thought to represent neural function (Merzenich, 2001). Further complicating matters, there has also been, in some quarters, a fragmentation of language with an emphasis on specific dominant components (e.g., sentence structure; see Chomsky, 1957).

Given this state of affairs, it may be useful to briefly review these models of language. First, to illustrate a widely used descriptive model of language, consider the following typical sentence: "The bear is running away." At the most basic level, this sentence includes speech sounds. For example, the word *is* includes a consonant sound /s/ and a vowel sound /i/. This aspect of language is defined descriptively as *phonology* (Camarata, 1991). In addition to speech sounds, this typical sentence also contains words (e.g., *the* and *bear*). Word meanings are defined as *semantics.* Although the scope of semantics can extend beyond individual words to include sentence meaning (e.g., Filmore, 1968), semantics generally applies to word level meaning (vocabulary). Some of the words also contain affixes (prefixes and/or suffixes). For example, the word *running* includes the root word *run* and the progressive suffix *ing*. The description of these affixes falls within the domain of the term *morphology.* Morphology also includes auxiliary and copula forms of the verb *be* (e.g., the auxiliary verb *is*) and function words such as *the*.

In addition to sounds and words, the sentence has a specific word order. It would be ungrammatical to say, "is bear the away running." This aspect of oral language is known as *syntax,* which includes a description of the rules for arranging words into sentences. Another name for the combination of syntax and morphology that may be more familiar to educators is the term *grammar.* As with the terms *articulation* and *phonology,* the combination of syntax, morphology, and grammar is synonymous (Pinker, 1999). Finally, the previously mentioned typical sentence occurred within a social and linguistic context (e.g., providing an example within this article). The social context in which a sentence appears is defined as *pragmatics*. In order to illustrate how pragmatics applies to oral language, consider the sentence "Can you close the door?" in two different contexts. In the first context, imagine that the sentence is spoken to a student sitting next to an open door. In this example, the sentence is a request (e.g., to close the door). Conversely, imagine that a patient is receiving physical therapy, and the therapist is trying to determine the extent of the patient's residual physical capabilities. In this example, the previous question is interpreted literally (e.g., are you able to close the door?). In each of these examples, the phonology, semantics, morphology, and syntax are precisely the same, yet the sentence means different things based on its context.

It should be noted that pragmatics has only recently appeared on the measurement of language scene (cf. Prutting & Kirshner, 1987), and there are few standardized assessments available to directly evaluate this aspect of language. However, it will become increasingly important within assessment because the ultimate communicative success of language users is predicated on using language correctly within a shifting social context. The differential diagnosis of some language-related conditions (e.g., autism and mixed expressive–receptive language disorders) is partially predicated on the ability to differentiate verbal and nonverbal social responsivity (pragmatics) based on disruptions in the ability to comprehend language as opposed to a psychiatric condition wherein a child resists or avoids social interaction (Kanner, 1943; Koegel & Koegel, 1995). Thus, accurate verbal and nonverbal measures of pragmatics will be useful. Moreover, within a descriptive framework, language is defined as a code for conveying ideas, with the code including phonology, semantics, morphology, syntax, and pragmatics. Finally, a question to address here is whether this particular definition has any advantages over explanatory or component-specific definitions of language. One can argue that the construct validity of any of the competing models of language is directly related to the degree to which the model captures actual language behavior. Figure 1 presents a schematic of this descriptive model of language.

This model has proven very useful in analyzing and classifying world languages (Bloomfield, 1933) and in diagnosing and treating language disorders in children (Camarata, 1991; Paul, 1995). One could argue that the reported utility in diagnosis and treatment is because this orientation is derived from direct observation of a child's language in real, everyday contexts (Ingram, 1989; Miller, 1981) and because the focus of treatment derived from these analyses focuses on the integrated, functional use of each area (phonology, semantics, etc.) in a useful social context (e.g., home or school). But one could also argue that observational measures of this nature are difficult to elicit in a standardized manner and are inherently

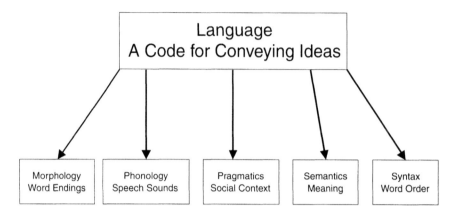

Figure 1. A descriptive model of language.

more susceptible to bias (Salvia & Ysseldke, 1995). Perhaps more importantly, this model is useful precisely because it focuses squarely on what a child uses to communicate and may reduce reliance on diagnosis and treatment based on special skills that bear little correspondence to functional abilities and special treatments that improve one or more of these special skills but often have no impact on a child's language at home or in school (Fuchs & Fuchs, 2001). But one could also argue that gross classification of language into five descriptive domains is superficial in terms of underlying cognitive processes (R. Woodcock, personal communication, March 2002). Although there is a healthy tension between functional outcome and measurement specificity, it may be useful to discuss language abilities in terms of recent advances in measurement of cognitive abilities and then integrate this model with the more functional, descriptive view described previously.

As noted earlier in this article, there has been significant interest in describing the cognitive and neural aspects of language (Miller, 1951; Osgood, 1971). The Illinois Test of Psycholinguistic Abilities (Kirk, McCarthy, & Kirk, 1968) was an early effort to measure language abilities within this theoretical framework. Within this conceptualization, language is considered as a series of input and output processes. Although one could argue that this instrument was psychometrically sound (McCauley & Swisher, 1984) and that many items have seen new life in more recent and widely used tests (e.g., the Test of Language Development–Primary 3; Hammill and Newcomer, 1998), the reliance on nonfunctional items (e.g., repetition of digits) provided limited utility for intervention. That is, although repeating a string of numbers likely has diagnostic value (Schrank et al., 2002), in that this task may distinguish language disordered and nonimpaired populations, teaching a child to repeat digits does not necessarily improve expressive or receptive language abilities.

Language Abilities and General Cognitive Assessment

Language abilities are one of the fundamental constructs within an intellectual or achievement battery (Schrank et al., 2002). For example, Carroll's three-stratum theory of human cognitive abilities (Carroll, 1993, 1998) includes language as an explicit component in Stratum I and as embedded components in Strata II and III. This has important implications in how these types of instruments are applied to children with language disorders. As a prelude to discussing these implications, it may be useful to review Carroll's model as an example of this kind of measurement. Table 1 includes a review of the strata for cognitive abilities (adapted from Schrank et al., 2002).

From an assessment perspective, consider which areas within Stratum I directly include language abilities as defined in the descriptive model (morphology, phonology, pragmatics, semantics, and syntax). Clearly, lexical knowledge, language development, and general (verbal) information would be language skills; lexical development and verbal information could be classified as one aspect of meaning (semantics), which together form the Stratum II construct of comprehension–knowledge. Similarly, speech–sound discrimination and phonetic coding would be aspects of phonology and comprise two of the three Stratum I abilities that are included in the Stratum II construct of auditory processing. Finally, semantic processing speed and naming faculty (also aspects of semantics) are two of the three Stratum I skills that are part of Stratum II processing speed. Thus, three of the seven Stratum II constructs that contribute to general intellectual ability directly are founded on phonological or semantic abilities.

In terms of indirect relationships between language ability and Stratum II constructs, it may be useful to examine the nature of the Stratum I items that contribute to the four Stratum II constructs that are not as clearly related to the descriptive model of language. Consider, for example, the relationship between language ability and visual–spatial thinking. One may assume that visual–spatial thinking is a language-free or, at the least, minimal-language construct. Tests designed to assess visual–spatial thinking in the Carroll (1993) model include visualization, spatial relations, and spatial scanning. Language faculty does not appear here. But

111

Table 1

Carroll's (1998) Three-Stratum Model of Cognitive Ability

Stratum I	Stratum II	Stratum III
Lexical knowledge and language development	Comprehension– knowledge	
General (verbal) information		
Associate memory	Long-term retrieval	
Ideational fluency		
Visualization	Visual–spatial thinking	All stratum II
Spatial relations		skills are
Spatial scanning		combined to
		yield "general
		intellectual
		ability"
Speech–sound discrimination	Auditory processing	
Resistance to auditory stimulus distortion		
Phonetic coding		
Induction	Fluid reasoning	
Sequential reasoning		
Semantic processing speed	Processing speed	
Perceptual speed		
Naming faculty		
Memory span	Short-term memory	

Note. Adapted from *Essentials of WJIII cognitive abilities assessment,* by F. Schrank, D. Flanagan, R. Woodcock, and J. Mascolo, 2002, and *Human cognition abilities: A survey of factor analytic studies,* by J. Carrol, 1993.

let's consider how spatial thinking is actually assessed. In one widely used and well-normed test of cognitive abilities (Woodcock–Johnson–III; Woodcock, McGrew, & Mather, 2001), visual–spatial thinking is assessed using a combination of spatial relations (subtest 3) and picture recognition (subtest 13). Picture recognition in this battery does include verbal instructions, but one could argue that if a pointing mode is used in responding, verbal mediation of this subtest is minimal. Indeed, this subtest appears to have been designed to restrict verbal mediation as a strategy for recalling the pictures presented (Woodcock et al., 2001). Spatial relations require a child to identify two or three pieces that combine to form a target shape (Schrank et al., 2002, p. 33). A child responds verbally by using a letter designation of the pieces. Although this clearly requires less expressive language than picture naming (obviously a semantic task), a child must know alphabetic designations. However, a child is permitted to point to the response items if he or she does not (or cannot) verbalize them. In contrast, comprehending the instructions also requires at least minimal receptive language ability, including syntax, morphology, and semantics. To be sure, the sample items will determine whether a child is comprehending the instructions presented in the introduction, but one could argue that some verbal faculty, at least in terms of receptive language, is needed to successfully complete these items. The point here is not to criticize the Woodcock–Johnson test, which is an excellent, well-normed, and useful instrument. Rather, this analysis is designed to illustrate that results on constructs that are relatively low in terms of verbal mediation actually may include some language faculty.

Perhaps another way to make this point is to consider the following scenario. Assume that the cognitive test is administered to someone who is of at least average intelligence but does not speak English. If the test were administered, how would this person perform? It is not surprising that one would expect this non-English speaker to perform quite poorly on many subtests and many of the Stratum I constructs, which, in turn, would effect the estimates of Stratum II skills and, ultimately, Stratum III, the estimate of overall cognitive ability. This simple truth is recognized by test makers who norm and distribute tests in multiple languages. But what if a child has a receptive language disorder that includes a limited lexicon (semantics) and difficulty understanding word endings (morphology) and complex sentences (syntax)? Further assume that these clinical deficits are amenable to intervention so that, like the non-English speaker learning English, comprehension could be established.

If language competence increased through intervention so that a larger vocabulary is learned, word endings are comprehended, and complex instructions can be understood, no one would be surprised if scores on the Stratum II domains of comprehension–knowledge, auditory processing, and processing speed increased and, hence, the ultimate estimate of Stratum III, general cognitive ability, increased. A less obvious outcome would be that the other Stratum II domains that require at least minimal language comprehension skills could also increase: Long-term retrieval, visual–spatial thinking, fluid reasoning, and short-term memory might also be effected. An interesting test of this question would be to complete pre- and posttesting with an instrument within a treatment paradigm designed to increase receptive language abilities. That is, a group of individuals with receptive language disorders could be taught vocabulary, grammatical markers, and comprehension of complex sentences. Note that the procedures for this training should not be to teach the test items that comprise Stratum I to avoid confounding the relationship; rather, the teaching should be functional comprehension of these skills. It would be interesting to determine whether increases in functional comprehension would be associated with gains in general intellectual ability as mediated by incidental increases in the Stratum I and II scores. This would be similar to gains seen when an adult learner with at least average cognitive ability completes the cognitive abilities test before and after learning to understand English. One could argue that it is unreasonable to argue that this adult had low cognitive abilities or academic potential prior to learning English. Bear in mind that one would not teach this mythical adult to speak English by having this person discriminate speech sounds, match shapes, recall dissociated word strings, identify digit strings or repeated patterns, or rotate shapes. Rather, they would be taught the pronunciation, vocabulary, morphology, syntax, and social use of English more directly.

Practical Implications

The practical implications of this analysis suggest that the functional receptive language skills of any student evaluated with a test of cognitive abilities should be considered when using these measures to estimate ultimate cognitive capability (Camarata & Swisher, 1990). The latent cognitive ability of this type of child may be grossly underestimated if this is not considered. There are numerous cases of children initially believed to have low-cognitive ability who ultimately were scored average or even above average when their language skills improved (e.g., Sowell, 2001).

A second implication is that overall functional language faculty should be considered when teaching a child with receptive language disorders to comprehend English. One of the ultimate goals of intervention should be to increase a child's ability to understand everyday instructions in the classroom and ensure that at least the rudimentary skills that allow for more detailed cognitive assessment are acquired. Again, we note that this does not mean teaching a child the items on the test battery that are included on Stratum I. To be sure, there can be overlap for a skill, such as lexical knowledge, wherein pictures are used to teach a child new vocabulary items. But the goal should be general comprehension skills that will allow a child to eventually have sufficient receptive language to cooperate with the assessment (and to learn in the classroom) so that an accurate and stable estimate of general cognitive ability can be obtained.

Finally, it may be useful to bear in mind the analogy of teaching someone new to the language to speak English. The ultimate goal of this kind of endeavor is to teach the functional use of the language in various contexts (conversation, text, everyday situations, technical exchanges, etc.). It is rarely the goal of such instruction to boost scores on Strata I, II, or III for general cognitive abilities. Although one could argue that being able to acquire multiple languages is perhaps an indicator of general cognitive ability, it is generally understood that acquiring English unto itself does not directly increase cognitive potential. It is also important to bear in mind that teaching a child to perform well on the language-related skills in Strata I and II will not automatically improve functional language in the classroom or in the community. Indeed, when presented with a language disorder case, the teacher or the clinician should always bear in mind that this latter domain is the ultimate goal of treatment.

Conclusions

The assessment of cognitive abilities is a useful and important activity. A comprehensive assessment using a well-normed and valid instrument (Woodcock et al., 2001) will yield important insights into a child's overall ability and the strengths and weakness in the various processes that contribute to cognitive ability (Schrank et al., 2002). Newly developed measures provide fresh data and additional potential applications and may ultimately provide a window into neuropsychological function. However, children with disabilities that include language disorders, particularly a receptive language disorder, require some thought when interpreting the results of these measures. The impact of the reduced language ability on testing should be thoughtfully considered, as should the developmental effect of language comprehension (Walters & Chapman, 2000) on related abilities in cognitive assessment. In addition, treatment for these disorders should include continual focus on the ultimate functional use of the language skills in school, home, and community contexts. Finally, it cannot be assumed that systematically teaching the skills used to sample the various language-related strata will automatically improve language ability or general cognitive ability.

References

Bloom, L., & Lahey, M. (1978). *Language development and language disorders.* New York: Wiley.

Bloomfield, L. (1933). *Language.* New York: Holt, Rinehart & Winston.

Camarata, S. (1991). Assessment of oral language. In J. Salvia & J.Ysseldyke (Eds.), *Assessment in special and remedial education* (pp. 263–301). Boston: Houghton Mifflin.

Camarata, S., & Swisher, L. (1990). A note of intelligence assessment within studies of specific language impairment. *Journal of Speech and Hearing Research, 33,* 205–207.

Carroll, J. (1993). *Human cognitive abilities: A survey of factor-analytic studies.* Cambridge, MA: Cambridge University Press.

Carroll, J. (1998). Human cognitive abilities: A critique. In J. McArdle & R. Woodcock (Eds.), *Human cognitive abilities in theory and practice* (pp. 5–24). Mahwah, NJ: Lawrence Erlbaum Associates, Inc.

Chomsky, N. (1957). *Syntactic studies.* The Hague, The Netherlands: Mouton.

Filmore, C. (1968). The case for case. In E. Bach and R. Harms (Eds.), *Universals in linguistic theory.* New York: Holt, Rinehart & Winston.

Fuchs, F., & Fuchs, D. (2001). Helping teachers formulate sound test accommodation decisions for students with learning disabilities. *Learning Disabilities Research and Practice, 16,* 174–181.

Hammill, D., & Newcomer, P. (1998). *Test of Language Development–Primary 3.* Austin, TX: Pro-Ed.

Ingram, D. (1989). *Phonological disability in children.* New York: Cole and Whurr.

Kanner, L. (1943). Autistic disturbances of affective contact. *Nervous Child, 2,* 250.

Kirk, S., McCarthy, J., & Kirk, W. (1968). *Illinois Test of Psycholinguistic Abilities.* Champaign, IL: University of Illinois Press.

Koegel, R., & Koegel, L. (1995). *Teaching children with autism: Strategies for initiating positive interactions and improving learning opportunities.* Baltimore: Brookes.

McCauley, R., & Swisher, L. (1984). A psychometric review of speech and language test. *Journal of Speech and Hearing Disorders, 49,* 34–42.

Merzenich, M. (2001). Cortical plasticity contributing to child development. In J. McClelland & R. Siegler (Eds.), *Mechanisms of cognitive development: Behavioral and neural perspectives. Carnegie Mellon symposia on cognition* (pp. 67–95). Mahwah, NJ: Lawrence Erlbaum Associates, Inc..

Merzenich, M., Jenkins, W., Johnston, P., Schreiner, C., Miller, S., & Tallal, P. (1996). Temporal processing deficits of language-learning impaired children ameliorated by training. *Science, 271,* 77–81.

Miller, G. (1951). *Language and communication.* New York: McGraw-Hill.

Miller, J. (1981). *Assessing language production in children.* Baltimore: University Park Press.

Osgood, C. (1971). Where do sentences come from? In D. Steinberg & L. Jakobovits (Eds.), *Semantics* (pp. 497–529). Cambridge, England: Cambridge University Press.

Paul, R. (1995). *Language disorders from infancy through adolescence: Assessment and intervention.* St. Louis, MO: Mosby.

Pinker, S. (1999). *Words and rules.* New York: Basic Books.

Prutting, C., & Kirshner, D. (1987). A clinical appraisal of the pragmatic aspects of language. *Journal of Speech and Hearing Disorders, 52,* 105–119.

Salvia, J., & Ysseldyke, J. (1995). *Assessment in special and remedial education* (6th ed.). Boston: Houghton Mifflin.

Schrank, F., Flanagan, D., Woodcock, R., & Mascolo, J. (2002). *Essentials of WJIII cognitive abilities assessment.* New York: Wiley.

Sowell, T. (2001). *The Einstein syndrome.* New York: Basic Books.

Walters, D., & Chapman, R. (2000). Comprehension monitoring: A developmental effect? *American Journal of Speech Language Pathology, 9,* 48–54.

Woodcock, R., McGrew, K., & Mather, N. (2001). *Woodcock–Johnson–III tests of cognitive abilities.* Itasca, IL: Riverside Publishing.

PEABODY JOURNAL OF EDUCATION, 77(2), 117–136

Change Dynamics in Special Education Assessment: Historical and Contemporary Patterns

Daniel J. Reschly
Peabody College
Vanderbilt University

This article discusses historical and contemporary influences on changes in special education assessment, with emphasis on three persistent themes: accurate classification, fairness to minority students, and special education outcomes. Dunn's contributions to each of the themes are discussed, along with other influences such as legislation and litigation. Current dynamics leading to significant changes in special education assessment are discussed, particularly in the disability category of specific learning disabilities.

In this series of articles honoring the legacy of Lloyd Dunn, it is especially appropriate to focus on important themes in special education assessment over the last century. Dunn contributed significantly to the thought and practice regarding accurate classification, fairness to minority students, and program outcomes. Each of the themes represents persistent challenges with implications for assessment practices.

High- and Low-Incidence Disabilities

Prior to discussing the three themes that are the foundation for this article, we need to understand the nature of the different kinds of disabil-

Requests for reprints should be sent to Daniel J. Reschly, Professor of Education and Psychology, Box 328, Peabody College, Vanderbilt University, Nashville, TN 37203.

ities. Disabilities can be divided into two broad categories: (a) low-incidence disabilities that typically have a biological or organic foundation and (b) high-incidence disabilities that are best explained by a social system model because the symptoms cannot be directly associated with underlying biological anomalies (Mercer, 1979). Moreover, high- and low-incidence disabilities, as the names imply, occur at markedly different rates. High-incidence disabilities occur at 1% or more of the general student population. In contrast, low-incidence disabilities occur at a far lower rate in the general student population.

Of the 13 categories of disability recognized in the federal Individuals with Disabilities Education Act (IDEA; 1991, 1997, 1999), 4 are regarded as high-incidence disabilities: mild mental retardation (MR), emotional disturbance (ED), specific learning disabilities (SLD), and speech–language (Sp/L) disabilities. Collectively, they account for over 85% of all students with disabilities served in special education programs (see Table 1). Other key characteristics of persons with mild MR, ED, SLD, and Sp/L are as follows: (a) Identification usually occurs after school entrance subsequent to teacher referral and psychological and educational testing; (b) referrals typically are made due to low achievement, which is often accompanied by disruptive classroom behavior of varying severities; (c) reading problems are the primary or secondary reasons for about 75% to 80% of referrals; (d) incidence is positively correlated with poverty; and (e) persons with high-incidence disabilities are rarely officially identified as being disabled during their adult years, although symptoms and coping difficulties often are apparent in adult role performance (Koegel & Edgerton, 1984).

Before addressing the three themes, there are several other features of the distribution of disabilities that bear further comment (see Table 1). First, the most frequently occurring disability is SLD, which is diagnosed in nearly 6% of the school age population and accounts for over half of all students in special education. Second, the overall prevalence of SLD has increased by 250% since 1976. Many regard the current SLD prevalence rate of 5.73% as excessive. It certainly is far higher than the 2% figure suggested by leading figures when SLD was first being recognized as a special education category (Kirk, 1972). Excessive numbers of students with disabilities, particularly those classified as SLD, result in criticism of special and general education, focusing additional attention on the long-standing concerns about the effectiveness of special education programs (e.g., Dunn, 1968). The benefits of current special education programs for students with SLD are not well documented (Lyon et al., 2001), leading to advocacy for significant system reforms (see later discussion).

The long-standing and continuing concerns about the accurate classification of students with disabilities is apparent in the results reported in

Table 1

Prevalence of Students With Disabilities (SWD) in U.S. Schools, Age 6–17 (U.S. Department of Education, 2000)

Disability[a]	SWD Number Age 6–11	SWD Number Age 12–17	Total SWD Age 6–17	Percent of Disabilities[b]	Percent of Population[c]	Variations Between States[d]
SLD	1,113,465	1,603,190	2,716,655	50.5%	5.73%	3.1% (KY) to 9.6% (RI); (factor of 3.1)
Sp/L	955,505	126,317	1,081,822	20.1%	2.28%	0.9% (DC) to 3.7% (WV); (factor of 4.1)
MR	238,323	308,106	546,429	10.2%	1.15%	0.3% (NJ) to 2.87 (WV); (factor of 9.6)
ED	159,691	283,452	443,143	8.2%	0.94%	0.1% (AR) to 2.0% (MN); (factor of 20)
Low incidence	326,445	268,515	94,960	11.1%	1.26%	
All disabilities	2,793,429	2,589,580	5,383,009	100.1%	11.36%	9.2% (CA) to 16.5% (RI); (factor of 1.8)

Note. Compiled from data in the report *To Assure the Free Appropriate Public Education of All Children With Disabilities: Twenty-Second Annual Report to Congress on the Implementation of the Education of the Individuals With Disabilities Act,* by the Office of Special Education Programs, 2000, Washington, DC: U.S. Department of Education. Copyright 2000 by the U.S. Department of Education. Reprinted with permission.

[a]SLD = specific learning disabilities; Sp/L = speech–language disabilities; MR = mental retardation; ED = emotional disturbance; low incidence = combined total of multiple disabilities, hearing impairments, orthopedic impairments, other health impairments, visual impairments, autism, deafness or blindness, traumatic brain injury, and developmental delay. [b]Refers to the composition of the disability population. For example, of all students with disabilities age 6–17, slightly over half are in the category of SLD. [c]Refers to the risk level for each disability in the overall student population. For example, 5.73% of all students age 6–17 in the general student population have SLD. [d]Provides the lowest and highest prevalence of each disability by state and the multiplicative factor by which they differ.

the last column of Table 1. In this column, the variance between the highest and the lowest state prevalence of high-incidence disabilities is contrasted. Dramatic differences in prevalence are revealed. For example, SLD varies from a low of about 3% in Kentucky to a high of over 9.5% in Rhode Island. ED prevalence varies from an unrealistically low 0.1% in Arkansas to a more realistic 2% in Minnesota. There are no ready explanations for variations by factors of 3 and 20 in SLD and ED prevalence, respectively. It stretches credulity to posit that variations of that magnitude actually exist in the respective populations of those and the other states highlighted in the last column of Table 1.

Accurate Classification

The accurate classification of students with high-incidence disabilities is a persistent theme in special education assessment. Comparable issues with the classification of students with low-incidence disabilities either do not exist or the issues are very different. Specific practical issues, and increasingly over the last quarter century, legal requirements, have driven the development of assessment tools and approaches for classification. The advent of additional disabilities over the last century prompted expanded challenges and new assessment tools and approaches. In addition, changing conceptions of disabilities have an obvious influence on assessment practices.

Disability Conceptions and Criteria

Disability conceptions and criteria are related but not identical. The disability conception indicates the fundamental properties or underlying dimensions of behavior, while the classification criteria refer to how one is determined to be eligible for the disability diagnosis. Typically, early in the course of the recognition of a disability, conception and criteria are closely related. As the disability category is used over time, with accumulating research and more sophisticated means of assessment, the conception and criteria may diverge, leading to calls for the reforms or reconceptualization of the disability.

Two cases illustrate this point. The traditional conception of MR as a permanent status of the individual (Doll, 1941) was stretched ultimately to the breaking point by the use of the term *pseudofeeblemindedness* to account for the adults earlier diagnosed as MR who functioned within broad normal limits. Benton (1956) elucidated the irrationality of the use of this hackneyed term leading to, along with other influences, the modern conception of MR as referring to the current status of the individual without a specification of ultimate adult status (Grossman, 1973, 1983; Heber, 1959, 1961; Luckasson et al., 1992, 2002).

A similar phenomenon is underway with SLD. SLD typically is conceptualized as,

> . . . a disorder in one or more of the basic psychological processes involved in understanding or in using language, spoken or written, that may manifest itself in an imperfect ability to listen, think, speak, read, write, spell, or to do mathematical calculations, including conditions such as perceptual disabilities, brain injury, minimal brain dysfunction, dyslexia, and developmental aphasia. (IDEA, 1991, 1997, 1999; 34 CFR 300.7).

The problem with this conception of SLD is that current classification criteria rarely focus on the key feature of the definition—basic psychological processes (Mercer, Jordan, Allsopp, & Mercer, 1996). Moreover, the most common method of diagnosing SLD, the discrepancy between current intellectual functioning and achievement, has itself come under harsh criticism (Fletcher et al., 1998), thus creating conditions similar to those in MR in the 1950s and 1960s when there were rapid changes in conception and classification.

Intellectual Assessment

A vast and rich history exists about intellectual assessment that is beyond the scope of this discussion. Prior to the very early 1900s, efforts to develop reliable and valid measures of intellectual functioning were largely unsuccessful (Sattler, 2001). The relevant part of that history has to do with the purpose behind the development of the first successful intelligence test by Binet and Simon in the early 1900s. The fundamental problem was the need for an objective method to understand the cause of low achievement, whether that low achievement was due to lack of effort or lack of ability (Wolf, 1969). Special programs for students having significant difficulty with the general curriculum had developed by 1905 in Paris and several large U.S. cities, creating the need to differentiate between different kinds of low achievement. These special classes predated the development of the Binet–Simon method by a few years (Doll, 1962, 1967; MacMillan, 1982), giving lie to the charge that special classes for persons of low ability were created directly from the advent of IQ tests.

The Binet method of measuring intellectual ability spread with remarkable rapidity through the Western world. We may cite many reasons for why this innovation spread so rapidly, including the expansion of mandatory attendance laws that required school attendance of the less able (Fagan, 1992), concerns about the menace of persons with mild MR and the need to protect society from them (Smith, 1985), and the growing implementation of special classes for persons with mild MR necessitating the development of objective diagnostic methods (MacMillan, 1982). Moreover, the need for an objective method to identify persons with extraordinary talent was of increasing interest, particularly in light of the then prevailing Galtonian notions of the dominance of genetics in the determination of eminence (Sattler, 2001). Although family background clearly is related to precocious intellectual performance, Terman's use of the Binet method in longitudinal studies of giftedness led to the recognition that superior talent exists in all social classes, a significant factor in social and economic mobility over the past 80 years (Terman & Oden, 1959).

School Psychology and Individual Evaluation Practices

Several authors have commented on the association between the development of the psychological subspecialty of school psychology and the mandate for intellectual assessment in the schools for the purposes of classification of students with disabilities (Fagan, 1987a, 1987b; Sarason, 1975). Fagan's historical research on school psychology and special education established that the first person to use the title *school psychologist* was Arnold Gesell, who held a joint appointment at Yale University and the Connecticut State Board of Education from 1915 to 1919. Gesell's work over that period reflected the early combination of (a) individual study of children referred for academic problems, (b) frequent use of measures of intellectual functioning along with less formal methods of assessment, and (c) placement out of general education classrooms into special education classes or outright school exclusion based on the assessment results and professional judgment. According to records from Gesell's work in 1917–1919, about two thirds of the cases were diagnosed as "mentally deficient or feebleminded," with special class placement recommended for most (Fagan, 1987a, 1987b). Indeed, Gesell's work scope and activities would be easily recognizable to a school psychologist working anywhere in the United States today!

Greater classification accuracy was fostered by the advent of intelligence tests nearly a century ago. This advance bears special mention because of its significant influence on the course of special education and assessment practices today. The developmental trend is especially instructive. The need existed for an objective method to identify low achievement due to low ability. Special classes already existed in many cities. That need was met through the technological advance of intellectual assessment that was implemented almost immediately throughout the Western world. The nature of how that technology was applied, coupled with individual case study by psychologists and other professionals, established a pattern of services that continues today in the requirement of a full and individual evaluation prior to the placement of children in special education.

Individual Achievement Tests

The quality of individually administered achievement tests lagged far behind the development of intelligence tests. There have been well-standardized, comprehensive individual intelligence tests available for the last 80 years. Comparable development of individually administered achievement tests occurred much later, beginning in the early 1970s. Those developed earlier were not comprehensive (e.g., Wide Range Achievement Test) or were poorly standardized (Gray Oral Reading Test; Salvia & Ysseldyke, 1978).

The later development of comprehensive, psychometrically sound, and individually administered achievement tests can be explained by the same dynamics that prompted the much earlier development of intelligence tests. The need did not exist for such tests as long as special education for persons with high-incidence disabilities consisted primarily of special classes for children and youth with mild MR. Mild MR and special classes dominated special education to the early 1970s (Mackie, 1969). The need for better individually administered achievement tests was prompted by the increasing interest in the category of SLD in the 1960s and 1970s. Initially, SLD was diagnosed primarily through IQ tests to establish average or above intellectual functioning and measures of psychological processes (e.g., Kirk & Kirk, 1971). By the early 1970s, serious problems with the processing measures were increasingly identified and widely read, scathing critiques of processing measures and instruction were published (Hammill & Larsen, 1974, 1978). The rapidly growing field of SLD required some classification method that was objective and replicable across settings. Hence, underlying processes were abandoned in SLD classification and other features of the LD conception were emphasized, especially unexpected low achievement.

There are a number of ways to operationalize the concept of unexpected low achievement (e.g., age or grade expectations, responsiveness to high quality instruction). The method chosen by the special education community in the 1970s was a combination of achievement lower than what might be expected based on the level of intelligence and ruling out other causes such as sensory deficits, low motivation, cultural differences, ED, and MR. The procedure adopted in the federal Education of the Handicapped Act (EHA; 1975) regulations following acrimonious debate was the requirement of a " ... severe discrepancy between achievement and intellectual ability." This regulation continues in IDEA (1997, 1999).

Achievement tests with sufficient psychometric quality were essential to the use of the intellectual ability–achievement discrepancy (Reynolds, 1984, 1985). Discrepancy analysis is fraught with psychometric challenges analogous to the issues associated with profile analysis and difference scores. In order to overcome those problems, individually administered achievement tests with excellent reliability and validity were required as well as sound methods to determine the size of the discrepancy to meet the criterion of *severe*. Tests meeting these standards first appeared in the 1970s (e.g., Dunn & Markwardt, 1970), yielding another example of the dynamic between need and advances in special education assessment.

Legal Requirements for Assessment and Classification

The assessment provided to students with disabilities, particularly high-incidence disabilities, is one of the most tightly regulated areas of educational and psychological practice. Extensive legal regulations governing assessment in special education exist in the form of federal and state statutes, federal regulations and state rules implementing the statutes, court precedents, and quasi-legal advisory opinions and guidelines (Reschly, 2000). A full discussion of the legal requirements is beyond the scope of this article, but three features of legal requirements are important here.

First, the legal requirements reflect concerns with accurate special education eligibility determination (see especially the federal Protection in Evaluation and Eligibility Determination regulations at 34 CFR 300.530 through 300.543). Key regulations for the past 25 years include the requirements of full and individual evaluation, assessment instruments administered and interpreted by personnel with appropriate training, consideration of a wide range of information over multiple domains of functioning, explicit rejection of decisions made solely on the basis of IQ tests, mandatory periodic reevaluation, and decision making by a group of persons including parents. These regulations clearly were designed to prevent misclassification of persons with disabilities.

Second, legal regulations, particularly at the state level, mandate the use of specific assessment procedures. This mandate appears in different forms. One is the disability classification scheme adopted by the states, including the conceptual definitions and classification criteria. For example, the SLD classification criteria in most states, following the federal regulations, require the existence of a large discrepancy between intellectual ability and academic achievement in one or more areas (e.g., reading, mathematics, written language). Schools are essentially required to use individually administered tests of intellectual ability and achievement. Similarly, MR criteria nearly always require assessment of intellectual ability and adaptive behavior.

A third and more subtle feature is that trends in the provision of services to students with disabilities prompt changes in legal requirements regarding assessment. In the 1991 IDEA reauthorization of the EHA of 1975, a mandate was added to provide transition services to students with disabilities no later than age 16 in order to improve early adult outcomes. Transitioning planning required more precise assessment of previously largely ignored areas such as vocational interests and aptitudes, work related social behaviors and attitudes, and self-determination competencies. Another example is the emphasis on preschool assessment prompted by the expanded age ranges covered by the IDEA.

Current Legal Trends and Disability Assessment

Two current trends are important in changing assessment practices. Accountability demands in recent legislation established mandates that all students, including students with disabilities, are educated in the framework of high standards, challenging assessments of achievement in relation to standards, accompanied by rewards or sanctions related to level of performance. These mandates are likely to be even more prominent in the reauthorization of IDEA that is anticipated in 2003. The use of accommodations for students with disabilities so that they can participate in high stakes assessments is emphasized; however, the accommodations are not supposed to undermine the validity of the test (Fuchs, 2002). The accountability demands are likely to prompt greater emphasis on assessment that is directly related to producing higher achievement (Shinn, 1998).

Discipline with students with disabilities is a second arena of recent legal change that has prompted changes in assessment. IDEA (1997, 1999), reacting to court decisions (e.g., *Honig*, 1988), mandated functional behavioral assessment and positive behavioral supports for students with disabilities who also had challenging behaviors in school settings (Tilly, Knoster, & Ikeda, 2000). The recent IDEA discipline requirements have obvious outcomes, greater emphasis on behavioral assessment methods, functional analysis of the causes of behavior problems, and implementation and evaluation of positive behavior supports.

SLD

The classification criteria for SLD are likely to change in the next reauthorization of IDEA, although any change will be intensely debated among the advocacy groups. The major problems with current SLD classification practices are as follows: (a) weak relationships to interventions (i.e., what needs to be taught, how to teach, and monitoring progress); (b) high costs coupled with questionable benefits; (c) invalid, poor readers with higher IQs and those with IQs consistent with reading levels do not differ in kind of instruction needed nor in response to instruction, at least for those students with IQ > 80 (Fletcher et al., 1998); (d) harmful practices because treatment for young children is delayed until 3rd or 4th grade rather then beginning in 1st grade when reading and other learning disabilities are first apparent (Lyon, et al., 2001; Vellutino, Scanlon, & Lyon, 2000); and (e) practices are no more accurate than alternatives that have closer relationships to interventions (Reschly, Tilly, & Grimes, 1999; Tilly, Reschly, & Grimes, 1999).

The National Joint Committee on Learning Disabilities (NJCLD) recently advocated the abandonment of the intellectual ability–achievement discrepancy, a major step in changing SLD classification criteria because it represents 10 organizations and 350,000 parents, teachers, professionals, and related services personnel (Learning Disability Roundtable, 2002). The NJCLD statement is similar to the recommendations of a National Academy of Sciences panel regarding minority overrepresentation (Donovan & Cross, 2002).

Accurate classification is a persistent theme in special education assessment. The need for accurate classification of students with high-incidence disabilities was a major influence on the development of the first successful intelligence test as well as the first individually administered, psychometrically sophisticated, comprehensive achievement tests. The challenge of accurate classification continues today as one of the major influences in special education assessment. As disability conceptions and classification criteria change along with shifting trends in services to students with disabilities, further changes in special education assessment practices can be expected.

Minority Representation and Classification Fairness

The overrepresentation of certain minority students in special education along with the suggestions that special education placement may be ineffective or even harmful are arguably the most controversial subjects in special education today. Both issues were highlighted in one of the most widely cited articles in special education literature (Dunn, 1968). The following quote from that article is often used and frequently misinterpreted in critiques of special education by minority critics.

> In my judgment, about 60 to 80 percent of the pupils taught by these teachers are children from low status backgrounds—including Afro-Americans, American Indians, Mexicans, and Puerto Rican Americans; those from nonstandard English speaking, broken, disorganized, and inadequate homes; and children from other non-middle class environments. (p. 6)

This statement is often misinterpreted as indicating that 60% to 80% of all minority students are in self-contained special classes for persons with mild MR, or that 60% to 80% of the students in those classes are minority students. Both assertions are egregious misquotations. In fact, Dunn merely asserted that students in classes for mild MR were largely from low social status backgrounds (a true statement; MacMillan & Reschly, 1998; Richardson, 1981). It is likely that many citations to Dunn (1968) have been by writers who did not go beyond the title, producing many misrepresentations about what was advocated regarding general education programming for students with disabilities, overrepresentation, and what now is called full inclusion.

Two critical matters are often misunderstood regarding minority representation in special education. First, the major issue in Dunn (1968) was not overrepresentation per se; rather, the critical issue was the effectiveness of self-contained special classes for persons diagnosed as mild MR and the need to consider other general and special education alternatives for these students. The evidence to 1968 suggested skepticism about the effectiveness of self-contained special classes (Johnson, 1962), a picture that is modified only slightly today (Kavale & Forness, 1999). Overrepresentation is not a concern in educational programs that are perceived as less stigmatizing and more effective (e.g., Head Start), even though the degree of overrepresentation is larger and involves greater numbers of children. Overrepresentation is not the problem; rather, the problem is overrepresentation in stigmatizing classifications and placement in programs with dubious benefits. Dunn clearly understood that.

A second major issue in the overrepresentation discussion is widespread misunderstanding of the basic data. Consider this example. Black students constitute 17% of the general student population and 35% of students with MR placed in special education. What percentage of Black students are in special education due to the MR classification? Invariably, professionals in special education and related areas, including school psychology, provide wildly inaccurate estimates such as 35%, 17%, and so on. In fact, of all Black students, only 2.6% are placed in special education due to the category of MR (compared to 1.1% of White students; MacMillan & Reschly, 1998; see Table 2).

The overrepresentation statistics are confusing to many. There are two statistics. The first, composition, refers to the makeup of a group. For example, in Table 2, the makeup of general education students is about 17% Black. The makeup of the category of ED is about 26% Black. Black students are overrepresented. But does this mean that a large proportion of Black students are in the ED category? The statistic that addresses this question is the risk index. The risk index refers to the proportion of students in a particular group who are classified in a specific category. For example, the risk of being classified as ED is .016; that is, 1.6% of all black students are classified as ED and placed in special education. Although both statistics relate to a different aspect of representation, the composition index often is misinterpreted, and the degree of overrepresentation is markedly exaggerated.

Several patterns in Table 2 are noteworthy. First, overrepresentation occurs in only 3 of the 13 categories: MR, ED, and SLD. Second, not all minority groups are overrepresented. Overrepresentation occurs in MR and ED for Black students and in SLD for American Indians. Hispanic students, contrary to widespread beliefs, are not overrepresented in special education! Moreover, Asian Pacific Islander students are markedly underrepresented. A largely unexplored and highly volatile question is whether this degree of disproportionality is actually inappropriate given what is known about the effects of poverty and the academic and behavioral profiles of children from poverty circumstances (Donahue, Finnegan, Lutkus, Allen, & Campbell, 2001; West, Denton, & Reaney, 2000).

The impact of the overrepresentation issue on special education assessment hardly can be overstated (Reschly, 1997, 2000). The litigation concerning this issue in the late 1960s and early 1970s (*Diana*, 1970; *Guadalupe*, 1972; *Larry P.*, 1972, 1974) exerted a profound influence on the EHA in the mid-1970s, particularly the Protection in Evaluation Procedures section (34 CFR 300–530 through 300.543). Those requirements established a number of protections against misclassification of students as disabled (see prior section). Moreover, the use of IQ tests in classification decisions

Table 2

Results Compiled from U.S. Department of Education (2000) Representation for Three Disability Categories

	Native American Indian		Asian Pacific Islander		African American		Hispanic		White	
	Composition	*Risk*	*Composition*	*Risk*	*Composition*	*Risk*	*Composition*	*Risk*	*Composition*	*Risk*
MR	1.1%	1.2%	1.7%	0.6%	8.9%	0.8%	34.2%	2.6%	54.1%	1.1%
ED	1.1%	1.0%	1.0%	0.3%	9.8%	0.7%	26.4%	1.6%	61.6%	1.0%
SLD	1.4%	7.3%	1.5%	2.3%	15.8%	6.5%	18.3%	6.6%	63.1%	6.1%
General education composition	1.1%		3.9%		14.9%		17.0%		62.7%	
Total SPED risk (13 categories)		13.1%		5.3%		10.6%		14.2%		12.1%

Note. MR = mental retardation; ED = emotional disturbance; SLD = specific learning disabilities; SPED = special education.

was challenged in ways not thought possible prior to a series of court cases (Reschly, Kicklighter, & McKee, 1988a, 1988b, 1988c). Most cases actually upheld the use of IQ tests as part of a comprehensive evaluation (*Marshall*, 1984, 1985); however, in *Larry P.*, IQ tests were banned in California with Black students if (and it was an important if) the outcome of IQ testing was diagnosis as educable mentally retarded and placement in special education classes that the trial judge characterized as dead-end and inferior (*Larry P.*, 1979). The court order was expanded in 1986 to ban all uses of IQ tests with Black students; then, after a curious sequence of events, the ban was rescinded in 1992 (*Larry P.*, 1986, 1992, 1994).

Judge Peckham's reasoning throughout *Larry P.* focused primarily on the harm to children from self-contained, special education classes that he described in scathing language. *Larry P.* was really about the effectiveness of special education programming, the same issue that Dunn highlighted in 1968 (Reschly et al., 1988c). In 1992, Judge Peckham clarified his reasoning, leaving no doubt that his main concern was with educational programming, not with IQ tests. He first remarked that the 1979 IQ testing ban was, ". . . clearly limited to the use of IQ tests in the assessment and placement of African-American students in dead end programs such as EMR" (*Larry P.*, 1992, p. 15). The point was made even clearer later in the 1992 order:

> Despite the Defendants' attempts to characterize the court's 1979 order as a referendum on the discriminatory nature of IQ testing, this court's review of the decision reveals that the decision was largely concerned with the harm to African-American children resulting from improper placement in dead-end educational programs. (*Larry P.*, 1992, p. 23)

A great deal more could be said about disproportionate special education placement. Interested readers are referred to Donovan and Cross (2002), MacMillan and Reschly (1998), and Reschly (1997). For the purposes of this article, it is sufficient to conclude that overrepresentation litigation and analyses of placement patterns have been a powerful dynamic that influenced assessment requirements embodied in federal regulations. These regulations are applicable to all children and youth considered for special education eligibility, ensuring the wide impact of overrepresentation issues. A more subtle, but, in the long run, more important influence of the overrepresentation issue has to do with heightened concerns about the effectiveness of special education programming and the relationship between special education assessment and program outcomes.

Program Outcomes and Changes in Assessment

The full case for significant changes in special education assessment cannot be made in this article, but interested readers are referred to Reschly, et al. (1999) and Reschly and Ysseldyke (2002). The basic argument for reform is that current assessment practices mandated in eligibility determination have little relationship to interventions. Moreover, current disability constructs have dubious reliability and validity, particularly treatment validity. For example, the educational needs and intervention principles across students with high-incidence disabilities are far more alike than different, undermining the argument that it is necessary to distinguish between mild MR, SLD, and ED. These observations have been made before (Heller, Holtzman, & Messick, 1982; Hobbs, 1975), but a set of studies funded by National Institute of Child Health and Human Development (NICHD) has brought renewed concern about the validity of current disability identification procedures.

The NICHD-funded studies on dyslexia (reading disability) have produced several conclusions that are now the cornerstone of Bush administration policies regarding general and special education (Lyon et al., 2001). First, there is a strong commitment to the implementation of scientifically based principles in general and special education programs. According to the NICHD studies on identification of students with SLD, the federal requirement of a severe discrepancy between intellectual ability and achievement is invalid and harmful:

> Classifications of children as discrepant versus low-achievement lack discriminative validity. . . . However, because children can be validly identified on the basis of a low-achievement definition, it simply is not necessary to use an IQ test to identify children as learning disabled. (Fletcher et al., 1998, p. 200)

This observation alone likely would be ignored by the special education community in light of the strong commitment of the SLD advocacy groups to the intellectual ability–achievement discrepancy criterion (Scruggs & Mastropieri, 2002). There is more, however. In fact, the discrepancy criterion causes harm: "For treatment, the use of the discrepancy models forces identification to an older age when interventions are demonstrably less effective" (Fletcher et al., 1998, p. 201). This observation is consistent with the experience of many practitioners and studies of placement data that reveal that students who are likely to have serious problems with learning to read can be identified early, perhaps by mid-kindergarten and certainly by the end of first grade. For technical reasons, it is difficult to meet the discrepancy criterion until third or fourth grade, delaying treatment for a crucial two or more years and compromising the likelihood of successful remediation.

The harmful effects of the SLD discrepancy criteria, as well as its questionable validity, have resulted in advocacy for abandonment of IQ and IQ-achievement discrepancy criteria as part of SLD eligibility determination by key Bush administration officials and by other professional groups (Learning Disability Roundtable, 2002). The impact of this change, if it occurs, is enormous. SLD accounts for over half of all students in special education. It is the softest category in that there are more potential disputes about eligibility than in any of the other 13 categories. The most likely replacement for current SLD eligibility criteria involves the combination of (a) low achievement relative to peers despite good classroom instruction and (b) insufficient response to interventions that meet rigorous quality standards carried out over a minimum of several weeks (Tilly, et al., 1999; Upah & Tilly, 2002).

System reform first recognizes that a number of intervention principles and programming elements are known to be effective with students with disabilities (Kavale & Forness, 1999). Many of these principles and programming elements are not incorporated in the vast majority of special education programs today, compromising potential program outcomes. Further, the assessment that typically is used in eligibility determination and in monitoring programs does not prompt or support the implementation of the principles related to positive outcomes. System reform advocates strongly endorse an *outcomes criterion,* meaning that priorities for eligibility criteria and assessment are based on the relationship of procedures to positive outcomes. The positive outcomes issue is fundamental to resolutions of the accurate classification and minority overrepresentation issues.

The advantages of the new SLD criteria and system reform programs are as follows: (a) emphasis is placed on interventions rather than internal child characteristics that have little to do with treatment, (b) rigorous problem-solving procedures are implemented that yield rich information from which effective special education programs can be developed, and (c) early intervention and prevention are emphasized rather than waiting until failure is sufficiently severe to meet eligibility discrepancy criteria. Moreover, virtually the same students are found eligible with the new criteria and the assessment procedures used to implement these criteria but with this important difference: Intervention is initiated sooner and the components of effective programs are established during eligibility determination. Examples of these elements are explicit definitions of target behaviors, establishment of ambitious goals, implementation of empirically validated instruction, monitoring progress frequently with instructional changes made based on child outcomes, and evaluation of effects with accountability for results (Reschly et al., 1999).

Several locations in the United States are implementing systems with these characteristics and are experiencing promising results (Reschly & Ysseldyke, 2002). The principal beneficiaries are children and youth with learning and behavior problems. The alternative criteria and system changes require considerable continuing education of current professionals, a major barrier to rapid, widespread adoption, but the skills and competencies are well established and transmittable to others using effective continuing education methods.

The alternative eligibility criteria and system reform themes are contemporary answers to perennial special education issues, accurate classification, minority overrepresentation, and program outcomes. Ensuring positive outcomes is the principal impetus for system change today. Absent positive outcomes, special education is not justifiable, as Dunn (1968) eloquently argued. The answers, albeit tentative and approximate, to the effective outcomes question today are based on principles known to be effective with children with learning and behavior problems and the adoption of assessment practices that support implementation of empirically validated principles. These changes are promising, but it is likely that the perennial special education issues regarding accurate classification, minority overrepresentation, and program outcomes will exist many decades into the future.

References

Benton, A. (1956). The concept of pseudofeeblemindedness. *Archives of Neurology and Psychiatry, 75*, 379–388.

Diana v. State Board of Education, No. C-70–37 RFP (U.S. District Court, Northern District of California, Consent Decree, February 3, 1970).

Doll, E. A. (1941). The essentials of an inclusive concept of mental deficiency. *American Journal of Mental Deficiency, 46*, 214–219.

Doll, E. E. (1962). Historical survey of research and management of mental retardation in the U.S. In E. P. Trapp (Ed.), *Readings on the exceptional child.* New York: Appleton-Century-Crofts.

Doll, E. E. (Ed.). (1967). Historical review of mental retardation 1800–1965: A symposium. *American Journal of Mental Deficiency, 72*, 165–189.

Donohue, P. L., Finnegan, R. J., Lutkus, A. D., Allen, N. L., & Campbell, J. R. (2001). *The nation's report card: Fourth grade reading 2000.* Washington, DC: U.S. Department of Education, National Center for Educational Statistics, Office of Educational Research and Improvement.

Donovan, M. S., & Cross, C. T. (2002). *Minority students in special and gifted education.* Washington, DC: National Academy Press.

Dunn, L. (1968). Special education for the mildly retarded: Is much of it justifiable? *Exceptional Children, 35*, 5–22.

Dunn, L. M., & Markwardt, F. C. (1970). *Peabody Individual Achievement Test*. Circle Pines, MN: American Guidance Service.

Education of All Handicapped Children Act of 1975, 20 U.S.C. §1400 *et seq.* (statute); 34 CFR 300 (regulations published in 1977).

Fagan, T. K. (1987a). Gesell: The first school psychologist, Part I. The road to Connecticut. *School Psychology Review, 16*, 103–107.

Fagan, T. K. (1987b). Gesell: The first school psychologist. Part II: Practice and significance. *School Psychology Review, 16*, 399–409.

Fagan, T. K. (1992). Compulsory schooling, child study, clinical psychology, and special education: Origins of school psychology. *American Psychologist, 47*, 236–243.

Fletcher, J. M., Francis, D. J., Shaywitz, S. E., Lyon, G. R., Foorman, B. R., Stuebing, K. K., et al. (1998). Intelligent testing and the discrepancy model for children with learning disabilities. *Learning Disabilities Research and Practice, 13*, 186–203.

Fuchs, L. S. (2002). Best practices in providing accommodations for assessment. In A. Thomas & J. Grimes (Eds.), *Best practices in school psychology* (4th ed., pp. 899–909). Bethesda, MD: National Association of School Psychologists.

Grossman, H. (Ed.). (1973, 1983). *Manual on terminology and classification in mental retardation*. Washington, DC: American Association on Mental Deficiency.

Guadalupe Organization v. Tempe Elementary School District No. 3, No. 71–435 (D. Ariz., January 24, 1972; consent decree).

Hammill, D., & Larsen, S. (1974). The effectiveness of psycholinguistic training. *Exceptional Children, 41*, 5–14.

Hammill, D., & Larsen, S. (1978). The effectiveness of psycholinguistic training: A reaffirmation of position. *Exceptional Children, 44*, 402–414.

Heber, R. (1959). A manual on terminology and classification in mental retardation. *American Journal of Mental Deficiency Monograph Supplement*, 64(2).

Heber, R. (1961). Modification of the "Manual on Terminology and Classification in mental retardation." *American Journal of Mental Deficiency*, 65(4), 499–500.

Heller, K., Holtzman, W., & Messick, S. (Eds.). (1982). *Placing children in special education: A strategy for equity*. Washington, DC: National Academy Press.

Hobbs, N. (1975). *The futures of children*. San Francisco: Jossey-Bass.

Honig v. Doe, 56 S. Ct. 27 (1988).

Individuals With Disabilities Education Act (1991, 1997, 1999). 20 USC 1400 *et. seq.* (statute); 34 CFR 300 (regulations), Regulations Implementing IDEA (1997) (*Federal Register*, 1999, March 12, 1999, vol. 64, no. 48).

Johnson, G. O. (1962). The mentally handicapped: A paradox. *Exceptional Children, 29*, 62–69.

Kavale, K. A., & Forness, S. R. (1999). Effectiveness of special education. In C. R. Reynolds & T. B. Gutkin (Eds.). *The handbook of school psychology* (3rd ed., pp. 984–1024). New York: Wiley.

Kirk, S. A. (1972). *Educating exceptional children* (2nd ed.). Boston: Houghton Mifflin.

Kirk, S. A., & Kirk, W. (1971). *Psycholinguistic learning disabilities: Diagnosis and remediation*. Champaign: University of Illinois Press.

Koegel, P., & Edgerton, R. B. (1984). Black "six hour retarded children" as young adults. In R. B. Edgerton (Ed.), *Lives in process: Mildly retarded adults in a large city* (pp. 145–171). Washington, DC: American Association on Mental Deficiency.

Larry P. v. Riles, 343 F. Supp. 1306 (N. D. Cal. 1972) (preliminary injunction), *aff'd* 502 F. 2d 963 (9th cir. 1974); 495 F. Supp. 926 (N. D. Cal. 1979) (decision on merits), *aff'd* (9th cir. no. 80–427 Jan. 23, 1984). Order modifying judgment, C-71–2270 RFP, September 25, 1986. Memorandum and Order (August 31, 1992), *aff'd* F. (9th Cir. 1994).

Learning Disability Roundtable (2002). Policy recommendations for the reauthorization of the Individuals with Disabilities Education Act (IDEA). Retrieved from http://www.nasponline.org/pdf/LDpolicyroundtable.pdf

Luckasson, R., Coulter, D. L., Polloway, E. A., Reiss, S., Schalock, R. L., Snell, M. E., et al. (1992). *Mental retardation: Definition, classification, and systems of support* (9th ed.). Washington, DC: American Association on Mental Retardation.

Luckasson, R., Brothwick-Duffy, S., Buntinx, W. H. E., Coulter, D. L., Craig, E. M., Reeve, A., et al. (2002). *Mental retardation: Definition, classification, and systems of support* (10th ed.). Washington, DC: American Association on Mental Retardation.

Lyon, G. R., Fletcher, J. M., Shaywitz, S. E., Shaywitz, B. A., Wood, F. B., Schulte, A., et al. (2001). Rethinking learning disabilities. In C. E. Finn, Jr., A. J. Rotherham, & C. R. Hokanson, Jr. (Eds.), *Rethinking special education for a new century* (pp. 259–287). Washington, DC: Thomas B. Fordham Foundation and Progressive Policy Institute.

Mackie, R. (1969). *Special education in the United States: Statistics 1948–1966.* New York: Teachers College Press.

MacMillan, D. (1982). *Mental retardation in school and society* (2nd ed.). Boston: Little, Brown.

MacMillan, D. L., & Reschly, D. J. (1998). The disproportionate representation of African-Americans in special education: The case for greater specificity or reconsideration of the variables examined. *Journal of Special Education, 32,* 15–24.

Marshall et al. v. Georgia, U.S. District Court for the Southern District of Georgia, CV482–233 (June 28, 1984), *aff'd* 11th Cir. No. 84–8771 (Oct. 29, 1985). (Appealed as *NAACP v. Georgia*). Note: the court of appeals decision was published as *Georgia State Conference of Branches of NAACP v. State of Georgia.*

Mackie, R. (1969). *Special education in the United States: Statistics 1948–1966.* New York: Teachers College Press.

Mercer, C. D., Jordan, L., Allsopp, D. H., & Mercer, A. R. (1996). Learning disabilities definitions and criteria used by state education departments. *Learning Disability Quarterly, 19,* 217–232.

Mercer, J. (1979). In defense of racially and culturally nondiscriminatory assessment. *School Psychology Digest, 8,* 89–115.

Reschly, D. J. (1997). *Disproportionate minority representation in general and special education programs: Patterns, issues, and alternatives.* Des Moines, IA: Mountain Plains Regional Resource Center, Drake University. (ERIC Document Reproduction Service No. ED415632)

Reschly, D. J. (2000). Assessment and eligibility determination in the *Individuals With Disabilities Act of 1997.* In C. F. Telzrow & M. Tankersley (Eds.), *IDEA amendments of 1997: Practice guidelines for school-based teams* (pp. 65–104). Bethesda, MD: National Association of School Psychologists.

Reschly, D. J., Kicklighter, R. H., & McKee, P. (1988a). Recent placement litigation, Part I: Regular education grouping: Comparison of *Marshall* (1984, 1985) and *Hobson* (1967, 1969). *School Psychology Review, 17,* 7–19.

Reschly, D. J., Kicklighter, R. H., & McKee, P. (1988b). Recent placement litigation Part II, Minority EMR overrepresentation: Comparison of *Larry P.* (1979, 1984, 1986) with *Marshall* (1984, 1985) and *S-1* (1986). *School Psychology Review, 17,* 20–36.

Reschly, D. J., Kicklighter, R. H., & McKee, P. (1988c). Recent placement litigation, Part III: Analysis of differences in *Larry P., Marshall,* and *S-I* and implications for future practices. *School Psychology Review, 17,* 37–48.

Reschly, D. J., Myers, T. G., & Hartel, C. R. (Eds.). (2002). *Mental retardation: Determining eligibility for Social Security benefits.* Washington, DC: National Academy Press.

Reschly, D. J., Tilly, W. D., III, & Grimes, J. P. (Eds.). (1999). *Special education in transition: Functional assessment and noncategorical programming.* Longmont, CO: Sopris West.

Reschly, D. J., & Ysseldyke, J. E. (2002). Paradigm shift: The past is not the future. In A. Thomas & J. Grimes (Eds.). *Best practices in school psychology IV* (4th ed., pp. 3–20). Bethesda, MD: National Association of School Psychologists.

Reynolds, C. R. (1984). Measurement Issues in Learning Disabilities. *Journal of Special Education, 18,* 451–475.

Reynolds, C. R. (1985). Measuring the aptitude-achievement discrepancy in learning disability diagnosis. *Remedial and Special Education, 6,* 37–55.

Richardson, S. (1981). Family characteristics associated with mild mental retardation. In M. Begab, H. C. Haywood, and H. Graber (Eds.), *Psychosocial influences in retarded performance, Vol. II* (pp. 29–43). Baltimore: University Park Press.

Salvia, J., & Ysseldyke, J. E. (1978). *Assessment in special and remedial education.* Boston: Houghton Mifflin.

Sarason, S. (1975). The unfortunate fate of Alfred Binet and school psychology. *Teachers College Record, 77,* 579–592.

Sattler, J. M. (2001). *Assessment of children: Cognitive applications* (4th ed.). San Diego, CA: Jerome M. Sattler Publisher, Inc.

Scruggs, T. E., & Mastropieri, M. A. (2002). On babies and bathwater: Addressing the problems of identification of learning disabilities. *Learning Disability Quarterly, 25,* 155–167.

Shinn, M. R. (Ed.). (1998). *Advanced applications of curriculum-based measurement.* New York: Guilford.

Smith, J. D. (1985). *Minds made feeble: The myth and legacy of Kallikaks.* Rockville, MD: Aspen Systems Corporation.

Terman, L. M., & Oden, M. H. (1959). *Genetic studies of genius, Vol. 5: The gifted group at midlife.* Palo Alto, CA: Stanford University Press.

Tilly, W. D., III, Knoster, T. P., & Ikeda, M. J. (2000). Functional behavioral assessment: Strategies for behavioral support. In C. F. Telzrow & M. Tankersley (Eds.), *IDEA amendments of 1997: Practice guidelines for school-based teams* (pp. 151–198). Bethesda, MD: National Association of School Psychologists.

Tilly, W. D., III, Reschly, D. J., & Grimes, J. P. (1999). Disability determination in problem solving systems: Conceptual foundations and critical components. In D. J. Reschly, W. D. Tilly, III., & J. P. Grimes (Eds.), *Special education in transition: Functional assessment and noncategorical programming* (pp. 285–321). Longmont, CO: Sopris West.

Upah, K. R. F., & Tilly, W. D., III (2002). Designing, implementing and evaluating quality interventions. In A. Thomas and J. Grimes (Eds.), *Best practices in school psychology* (4th ed., pp. 483–501). Bethesda, MD: National Association of School Psychologists.

U.S. Department of Education (2000). *To assure the free appropriate public education of all children with disabilities: Twenty-second annual report to Congress on the implementation of the education of the Individuals With Disabilities Education Act.* Washington, DC: Office of Special Education Programs.

Vellutino, F. R., Scanlon, D. M., & Lyon, G. R. (2000). Differentiating between difficult-to-remediate and readily remediated poor readers: More evidence against the IQ-achievement discrepancy definition of reading disability. *Journal of Learning Disabilities, 33,* 223–238.

West, J., Denton, K., & Reaney, L. M. (2000). *The kindergarten year: Findings from the early childhood longitudinal study, kindergarten class of 1998–1999.* Washington, DC: National Center for Educational Statistics.

Wolf, T. H. (1969). The emergence of Binet's conception and measurement of intelligence: A case study of the creative process. Part II. *Journal of the History of the Behavioral Sciences, 5,* 207–237.